FAITH in the Community

Sally Lynch

Hodder & Stoughton
A MEMBER OF THE HODDER HEADLINE GROUP

Acknowledgements

The publishers would like to thank the following for permission to reproduce copyright material in this volume:

HarperCollins Publishers Ltd for the extract from *The Lion, the Witch and the Wardrobe*, C S Lewis; the *Daily Mail* for 'When "life" hardly seems enough'; Heinemann Publishers Ltd for the extract from *The Jewish War*, Josephus (trans. G A Williamson, Penguin Classics 1959, 1969); the United Nations Office and Information Centre for the Universal Declaration of Human Rights and use of the UN symbol. Extract from *Jesus, Me and You*, Cliff Richard (Hodder & Stoughton) with permission. Scriptures quoted from the NIV published by Hodder & Stoughton, © International Bible Society 1973, 1978, 1984 with permission.

British Library Cataloguing in Publication Data
Lynch, Sally
    Faith in the Community
    I. Title
    291

ISBN 0-340-62039-0

First published 1996
Impression Number   10 9 8 7 6 5 4 3 2 1
Year   1999 1998 1997 1996

Copyright © 1996 Sally Lynch

All rights reserved. No part of this publication may be reproduced or transmitted in any form or by any means, electronic or mechanical, including photocopy, recording, or any information storage and retrieval system, without permission in writing from the publisher or under licence from the Copyright Licensing Agency Limited, of 90 Tottenham Court Road, London, W1P 9HE.

Typeset by Litho Link Ltd, Welshpool, Powys, Wales
Printed in Great Britain for Hodder & Stoughton Educational, a division of Hodder Headline Plc, 338 Euston Road, London NW1 3BH by Hobbs the Printers, Totton, Hampshire.

Copyright © 1996 by Sally Lynch. The Publishers grant permission for multiple copies of this page to be made for use solely within that institution.

CONTENTS

Teacher's Notes

A GROWING UP IN THE COMMUNITY

	Notes for the Teacher	5
	Wordlist	8
1	Myself	9
2	Changes	11
3	Rights and Responsibilities	13
4	Initiation	15
5	Rules	19
6	Religious Rules	21
7	Rules Gone Mad	23
8	Breaking Rules	25
9	Punishment	28
10	Capital Punishment	31

B WORKING IN THE COMMUNITY

	Notes for the Teacher	33
	Wordlist	36
1	Work and Me	37
2	What is Work?	39
3	Work in the Community	42
4	Vocation and Talent	51
5	People at work	53
6	Money	55
7	Religions and Wealth	57
8	Leisure	59
9	Religions and Leisure	61
10	A Balanced Life	64

C PEOPLE AROUND US IN THE COMMUNITY

	Notes for the Teacher	66
	Wordlist	69
1	People Around Us	70
2	Religious Prejudice	72
3	Sexual Prejudice	78
4	Racial Prejudice	80
5	Persecution and Faith in the past	82
6	Persecution Today	85
7	Oppression Today	87
8	Human Rights	89
9	Handicap	91
10	Living With People Around Us	96

Copyright © 1996 by Sally Lynch. The Publishers grant permission for multiple copies of this page to be made for use solely within that institution.

TEACHER'S NOTES

This material is designed for use with students at KS4 following courses in RE. The content deals with people as part of a community. It starts with students at their current stage of 'growing up' into the community and follows through issues and experiences of community that they will have to consider as they prepare to leave school and go to work in the community. It thus attempts to fulfil clause 1 of the Education Reform Act by promoting the spiritual, moral and cultural development of pupils, as well as helping to prepare them for 'the opportunities, responsibilities and experiences of adult life'. The material is also suitable for use as part of PSE courses. It emphasises the need for wholeness of life, including the spiritual or religious aspect. The units can be followed as a whole course, roughly one unit per term; or they can be used individually.

Four of the Cross-Curricular Themes are dealt with in the material, and it is also consistent with the requirements of most existing local Agreed Syllabuses at KS4. Some of the sheets are suitable for use with GCSE groups as stimulus or tasks for reflection and discussion.

THE SHEETS

The sheets can be used individually as a whole course or to supplement existing material in school-designed courses. Information sheets provide stimulus material for students and may be used on their own, or backed up by other resources in and out of school. The worksheets provide a variety of tasks for students, and are suitable for all abilities at the selection of the teacher. Some teachers may want to record the text of the sheets onto tape so that students with reading difficulties can use them on their own. The circumstances of some tasks are deliberately vague to allow teachers to evoke their required response, for example asking students to work individually, in pairs or in groups. In some places a worksheet is printed first, suggesting that it should be tackled before looking at information about the topic. Brief notes below explain each topic and suggest ways in which the sheets might be used, as well as possible additional resources. They are only starter ideas!

THE WORDLISTS

Each unit has a wordlist. These are designed to help pupils to spell important words correctly and to learn the meanings of words. Teachers may wish to use them as reference sheets available for pupils to look up words, or for pupils to copy out, or to be given to less academic pupils to keep for reference.

EXTRA RESOURCES

The information sheets provide the basic material that might be needed, and schools will have their own materials to supplement these. Suggestions are made for further book or video resources. However, it might also be helpful to make use of the local community, where this is possible. Although this is difficult in the time allocated to KS4 RE, many people are only too willing to come into school and work with pupils – but teachers should meet all visitors themselves first and be satisfied about their suitability for work with this age group.

Section A

GROWING UP IN THE COMMUNITY

NOTES FOR THE TEACHER

AIMS AND OBJECTIVES

Aims
- to study the changes that occur in the growing up process, the responsibilities taken on, and the young person's relationship to society;
- to relate this to relevant religious issues.

Objectives

Knowledge of:
- the initiation rites of a number of world faiths – especially Christianity (Confirmation and Believers' baptism);
- various aspects of legal responsibility at certain ages;
- the Ten Commandments, their relevance when given and for today;
- Jesus' teaching and that of other faiths on basic responsibility in society;
- reasons for, and types of, punishment today.

Understanding of:
- some conflicts within the adolescent;
- the importance of initiation ceremonies (religious and secular);
- the importance of rules in society and religions.

Ability to:
- reflect on own life so far;
- formulate and express an opinion clearly;
- reflect on important issues;
- research issues and report back clearly;
- relate issues discussed to local examples.

Experience of:
- role play;
- visiting speakers;*
- debate;*

* as chosen by school

CONTENTS

Wordlist

1. Myself
   Information Sheet 1: the Buddhist Wheel of Life
   Worksheet 1: the journey of life
2. Changes
   Information Sheet 2: changes in growing up
   Worksheet 2: my past and hopes
3. Rights and Responsibilities
   Information Sheet 3: rights and responsibilities secular and religious
   Worksheet 3: game
4. Initiation
   Information Sheet 4a: Christianity
   Information Sheet 4b: Hinduism and Judaism
   Information Sheet 4c: Sikhism, Buddhism and Islam
   Worksheet 4: initiation tasks
5. Rules
   Information Sheet 5: rules
   Worksheet 5: role plays
6. Religious Rules
   Information Sheet 6: examples
   Worksheet 6: tasks
7. Rules Gone Mad
   Information Sheet 7: examples and conventions
   Worksheet 7: discussion, local research tasks
8. Breaking Rules
   Information Sheet 8a and 8b: examples – secular and religious
   Worksheet 8: discussion tasks
9. Punishment
   Information Sheet 9a: types and purposes of punishment
   Information Sheet 9b: life in prison
   Worksheet 9: research on attitudes
10. Capital Punishment
    Information Sheet 10: basic information
    Worksheet 10: arguments to lead to a debate

Copyright © 1996 by Sally Lynch. The Publishers grant permission for multiple copies of this page to be made for use solely within that institution.

THE SHEETS

1 Myself

This section is designed to help students to start from 'where they are now' and to reflect back on their lives so far. It is suggested that the worksheet is completed first, encouraging students to think about their own journey of life. I usually introduce this by sharing part of my own journey, either in pictorial form (to give some ideas of symbols) or using 'artefacts' (the top off my christening cake!, first pair of school navy-blue knickers!, exam certificates etc.). Having completed the worksheet students then have something with which to compare the Buddhist wheel of life. It might be worth looking at the Wheel and talking about it before explaining to pupils what each part means.

The whole Wheel is held in the mouth of the Lord of death, showing impermanence. At the centre are the three animals which cause unhappiness and suffering (rooster – attachment; snake – hatred, pig – ignorance). The second circle shows the fates of those with good karma, moving up and those with bad karma, moving down. The third circle shows the six spheres of existence into which one might be reborn depending on one's actions in this life (heat and cold; hungry spirits; animals; demigods; devas; humans). The outer ring shows some of the actions and attitudes which lead to constant rebirth. Outside the wheel stands the Buddha, pointing to the moon. This symbolises the peaceful way of mind that is nirvana.

2 Changes

This section is designed to help young people to think about the changes that occur in growing up, and the conflicts between themselves and 'authority' as these happen. Much of the material is discussion based which encourages students to reflect on their own experiences. It can be covered in as much or as little detail as appropriate for the time available or students' abilities. A useful textbook to provide further stimulus for students or staff is *From the Cradle to the Grave*, by K. O'Donnell, published by Hodder & Stoughton, 07131 7591 5.

3 Rights and Responsibilities

This section helps students to see the rights that both society and religions give to young people as they 'come of age' and the accompanying responsibilities. The game is designed to lead to a discussion of these rights in British society. Religions will be dealt with in the next section.
Answers:
at 10: 1, 3   at 12: 27   at 14: 5, 7, 9
at 15: 11   at 16: 2, 13, 14, 15, 16, 17, 18, 26, 28
at 17: 4, 6   at 18: 8, 10, 12, 19, 20, 21, 22, 25
at 21: 23, 24

4 Initiation

This section deals with the coming of age ceremonies of each religion. It should be emphasised that the ceremony does not just take place at adolescence, but may take place at any age when one feels ready to accept the full responsibilities of the faith. Yet young people in religions do often take vows that they will live as an adult in the faith. There are a number of good books which will give extra information about these rites. *From the Cradle to the Grave*, (see above) has useful cartoon-strip formats for less able pupils. A number of videos are also available such as the Channel 4 *Believe it or not* series.

5 Rules

The role plays are deliberately placed before the information sheet so that pupils have to think about their own rules first. The method of role play will need to be carefully explained and students will need a time scale to work on. The role plays are laid out in such a way that they could be cut up and a different role play could be used with each group so that each can feed back and learn from each other. Experience shows that they need to know the difference between 'what is a rule?', and 'what is a thing we need to do?', especially in the Survival role play. The introduction to rules on the information sheet is very basic. To take an example from fiction, William Golding's *Lord of the Flies* (now available on video) provides an excellent introduction to the setting up of a set of rules – and later the way that they are broken. This might tie in well with the whole section.

6 Religious Rules

This section is purely an introduction to religious rules and thus necessarily superficial. It is hoped that students will be able to research further about one or more religion. To help with this, *Guidelines for Life*, by M. Thompson, published by Hodder & Stoughton, 0340 51950 9, will be useful, along with any good book about the basics of world faiths. Essentially it is the beliefs of each religion that are being studied. The cloze paragraphs in the worksheet are simple so that brief notes may be made. For Special Needs students the sheet could be enlarged onto A3 and a list of the missing words might be provided (in order, these are: teachings, Holy Book, initiation, Ten Commandments, Torah, Old Testament, Talmud, Jesus, love, Allah, creed, five, fast, once, eight, harmlessness, truth, people). Task 2 aims to help students to see that rules are not constrictive and that a religious faith affects a person's daily life deeply.

7 Rules Gone Mad

The idea of this section is to challenge students to consider the value of all rules and the ways that people make decisions – sometimes rules have to be broken. For more information about Bonhoeffer see the *Faith in Action* booklet published by RMEP.

8 Breaking Rules

There is a lot of scope here for involving the school's community policeman or woman in helping students' research and helping them to see the police in a positive light – if handled sensitively. For more information about the Howard League for Penal Reform, write to: 322 Kennington Park Road, London SE11 4JP, and for NACRO write to: 169 Clapham Road, London, SW9 0PU.

9 Punishment

In Information Sheet 9b, Michelle is not a real character, but the information is taken from real life. It might be possible to bring into school someone who has links with prisons – a JP, prison officer, member of the Board of Visitors etc. to help give students some insight. A group of men from a local prison once made a video for my students to tell them a little about prison life – the main message being, 'you don't want to end up here'. Some schools might have similar links. In Worksheet 9a more could be made of the quotations. There are videos available of the film of *Oliver* and the BBC production of *The Lion, the Witch and the Wardrobe*. Linked with 9b, the BBC video *Words into Action* has a very useful programme on 'Forgiveness' which lasts for about 20 minutes and includes an interview with Michael Saward – the London vicar. I have used the *Question Time* technique very successfully with, in our case, a school Governor, our community policeman, member of the Board of Visitors of a local prison and a priest. The only drawback with my particular guests is that all are Christians and so verbal punch-ups are limited!

10 Capital Punishment

This section is fairly straightforward. For more information about religious viewpoints, see *Guidelines for Life* (see above) and *Moral Issues in Six Religions*, ed. Owen Cole, published by Heinemann 0435 302 99X.

WORDLIST

Growing Up in the Community

This list will help you with the spellings and meanings of key words in this unit.

Baptism
Christian initiation ceremony

Bar Mitzvah
Jewish coming of age ceremony for boys

Bat Mitzvah
Jewish coming of age ceremony for girls

Candidates
People to be tested or who are going through a religious ceremony

Capital Punishment
the death penalty for certain crimes

Community
a group of people related together in some way

Compassion
an attitude of genuine concern for people

Confirmation
a Christian initiation ceremony, next stage from baptism

Convention
something that is normally done

Deterrent
a way of making an action look unattractive

Gurdwara
Sikh place of worship

Holy Spirit
Christian belief in the aspect of God present on earth through believers

Initiation
a ceremony that makes someone a member of a group

Protection
to look after someone/thing in possible danger

Qur'an
Muslim holy book

Reform
to change for the better

Responsibility
to be accountable for certain things

Retribution
to pay back for something

Secular
having nothing to do with religion

Scripture
the holy book(s) of a religion

Testimony
a believer telling others about their faith

Vindication
seeing that the law is kept

INFORMATION SHEET 1

GROWING UP IN THE COMMUNITY

Myself

Many people find it helpful to think of life as a journey. It helps them to see their way along the path, and to cope with the good and bad things that happen. If you look carefully at your journey, you will find that, like most people, you have some parts that might be called religious or spiritual. This might not seem very clear, but at times, such as when someone dies or when a baby is born, there are often hints of things beyond our understanding which involve our spiritual nature.

Some people have specific religious rituals at some stages in their lives, e.g. baptism in the Christian religion and Bar Mitzvah in the Jewish religion. Other people simply feel that there is more to life than day to day existence.

Buddhists think of life as a wheel. They believe that the aim of life should be to get free from the continual cycle of birth and death. The Wheel is a visual aid to help people see the consequences of their actions to avoid the pain caused by greed, hatred and ignorance, and to seek the freedom and happiness brought about by generosity, love and insight (karma).

For Christians too, there is a desire to do the best that they can. Some believe that the things that happen to them are sent by God to test them, others simply accept what happens and try to follow Jesus' teaching in each situation.

The Buddhist Wheel of Life. Each image within the Wheel represents one particular feature of life and the wheel as a whole shows how they are connected to one another.

Copyright © 1996 by Sally Lynch. The Publishers grant permission for multiple copies of this page to be made for use solely within that institution.

WORKSHEET I

GROWING UP IN THE COMMUNITY

Myself

> Who do you think that you are?

> What experiences have you had so far in your life?

1. Try to list all of the things that have happened to you that you think were important. (It doesn't matter if other people disagree.) E.g. birth, moving house, brothers and sisters, exams, getting your first bike, dog dying, broken arm playing football.

2. Sometimes these things might have meant that your life has changed course in some way. There may be other things that you have had to decide, or which have been decided for you, which have determined the course of your life (parents separating, moving town, choosing a school).
   a) How do you feel about these things?
   b) What symbols could you use to describe your feelings about these things? (In the picture road signs, weather symbols and faces have been used!)
   c) What sort of journey have you had in life?

3. a) Try to draw your journey of life as a roadway or some other journey. Use symbols to show times of decision and your feelings about things that have happened. There is an example to help you. Yours could be any shape.
   b) If you wish to, when you have completed your journey picture, show it to a friend and discuss your pictures.
   (i) Are your symbols similar?
   (ii) Are there any things which might be called religious?
   (iii) How would you like it to go on?

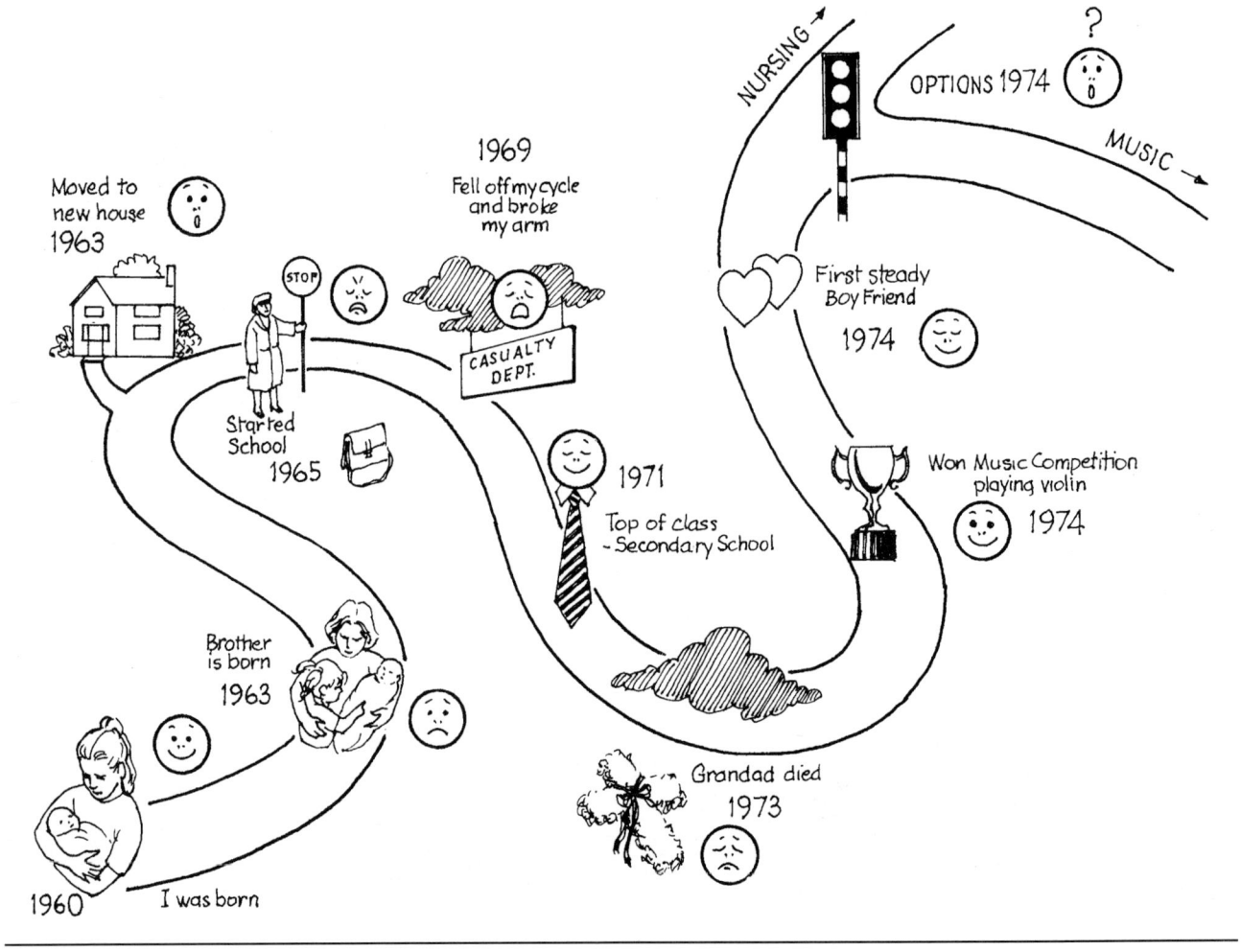

INFORMATION SHEET 2

GROWING UP IN THE COMMUNITY

Changes

As young people grow up they change. It's obvious, but it is important to remember that fact. It can help us to understand many of the conflicts that occur as we get older. This unit is about growing up into the community, but what is 'the community'?

A community is simply a group of people with whom we relate and of whom we are a part. We hear the word community a lot today, often used in the context of the town or area where we live – community centres are places where people in an area can go to get together for activities. Yet there are many types of communities, and as young people, we may belong to several at the same time.

A family is a community – a group of people who live and relate together. So is our school, church or religious group, youth club or football club, and on a wider scale our country is a community, and we are probably familiar with the term 'European Community' (EC) of which we are also a part.

Each community has its own rules and guidelines, accepted ways of doing things. These are regarded by 'members' as the 'norm', or, the normal way of doing things. These may be written or unwritten. As young people grow up they begin to question these guidelines and that can lead to conflicts. As we get older we want to think about why things happen and why we do things, we no longer take them for granted.

As our bodies change, so do our minds. We begin to think for ourselves, and we want to do things for ourselves. We may question why the older members of our communities do things the way that they do and this can lead to conflict. We are learning more about ourselves, and beginning to develop more confidence in ourselves, yet at times we also want to be able to retreat into the world of childhood for a break. It is an exciting time, but frustrating. Parents, teachers and others tell young people that they are 'too young to do that' and yet 'too old for that'. Sometimes it can be very confusing.

WORKSHEET 2

GROWING UP IN THE COMMUNITY
Changes

1. Think about the communities that you belong to. List them. Try to think about what the 'norms' are in each community. Compare your lists with a friend.

2. Now think about yourself as a Year 7 student. You could ask your friends, parents or teachers what you were like. List all of the ways that you have changed since then. There are some ideas around the edge of the page.

3. Using the above lists, consider in pairs the sorts of conflicts that might arise as you get older. Think about areas such as:

   - friends
   - clothes
   - religious life
   - the time you get in at night
   - the Law
   - homework
   - a career
   - money
   - helping at home
   - where you go
   - sexual attitudes
   - smoking and drinking

4. In groups, make up a play about one or more of the above conflicts. Try to draw in as many attitudes from the different characters as you can.

5. a) Discuss in groups how some of these situations of conflict might be sorted out.
   b) Look up the following Bible passages, and discuss whether they might be helpful in solving the conflicts, and how – for all people or just for Christians.

   Ephesians 6:1-4 Romans 13:1-10 Mark 12:29-31

6. You have already thought about yourself as a Year 7 student, and how you have changed. Now consider these questions carefully for yourself.

   - What are some of the best things about growing up?
   - What are some of the worst things?
   - What are some of the hardest decisions that you have had to make, or will make soon?
   - What are the worst conflicts that you have had?
   - What are your greatest hopes for the future?

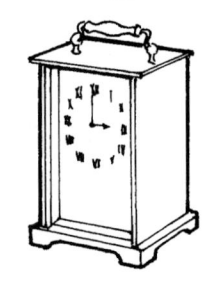

INFORMATION SHEET 3

GROWING UP IN THE COMMUNITY

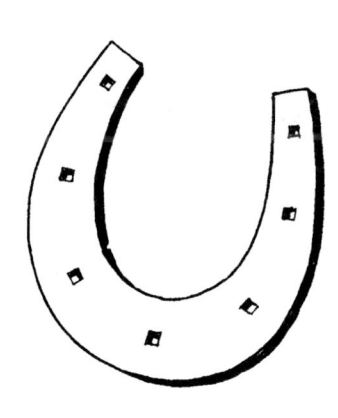

Rights and Responsibilities

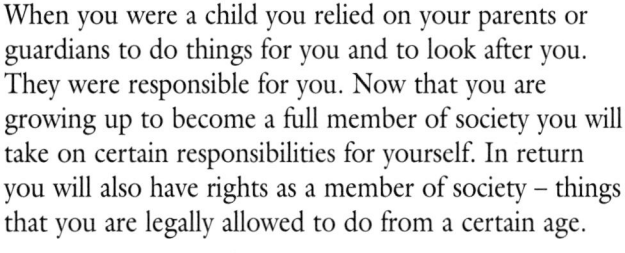

When you were a child you relied on your parents or guardians to do things for you and to look after you. They were responsible for you. Now that you are growing up to become a full member of society you will take on certain responsibilities for yourself. In return you will also have rights as a member of society – things that you are legally allowed to do from a certain age.

You will be allowed to vote for your local and national politicians and to have a say in who runs the country in which you live. In return you must be prepared to be called for Jury Service and help to run the system of justice and law in the country. You will be allowed to drive different vehicles, but you must take a test to prove that you are capable of doing so safely. You will be able to buy and drink alcohol, and to buy cigarettes. It is up to you then to use these things sensibly so that you do not abuse your body.

You will be expected to abide by all of the laws in this country. In the past your parents or guardians were responsible if you broke a law, now you must speak for yourself. You will be able to get married and to have a mortgage. In all of these rights, you will need to exercise responsible behaviour. As part of a community what you do and how you use your rights not only affects you – it can have a major effect on the people around you.

In the same way, in religious communities, young people are given certain rights as they get older. The religious community that they belong to will normally teach them as they grow up all that they need to know to be a full member of that religion. They will learn the ways of worshipping, the beliefs and teachings of their religion. Usually there will be a special ceremony at which the young person promises that they will be a faithful member of that religion, and some symbolic actions help to explain what is happening. Once they have been initiated into the religion, then the young people are able to take a full part in its life and worship. The age at which this takes place will vary both across and within religions.

In society there are set ages at which young people gain their rights.

WORKSHEET 3

GROWING UP IN THE COMMUNITY

Rights and Responsibilities

In this game you will match up the ages at which you are legally allowed to do certain things in Britain. You will need to work in groups of about five people. Each group should have a copy of this sheet. Cut it up so that you have a number of slips which have rights on. You will also have some smaller slips with ages on.

Place the AGE slips in a row on a desk. Shuffle the RIGHT slips and share them out to each person. Each person reads out in turn the RIGHT written on one of their slips. They must say at which age they think you are allowed this RIGHT and place it under that age slip.

The rest of the group may help out. Continue until all of the slips have been read out and placed under an age. Your teacher has the correct answers.

You might then like to discuss the correct answers:
- do you notice anything about the ages at which you can do a series of things (e.g. get married and get a mortgage or HP)?
- what responsibilities go with each of the Rights?
- do you think that any of these age restrictions are now outdated?

| 10 | 12 | 14 | 15 |
| 16 | 17 | 18 | 21 |

1 You can be arrested, detained, and sometimes searched and finger printed.	2 You must pay for dental treatment, eye tests and prescriptions unless in full time education, low income or pregnant.
3 You can be convicted of a criminal offence – but the prosecution must prove that you know the difference between right and wrong.	4 You can hold a full driving licence for all vehicles, except HGV and PSV.
5 You can be held fully responsible for a crime.	6 You can be sent to prison for serious crimes.
7 You can go into a pub and buy soft drinks.	8 You can get married without your parents' consent.
9 You must be responsible for wearing a seat belt in the rear seat of a car.	10 You can get a cheque card and a credit card.
11 Girls can be sent to a Young Offender Institution.	12 You can vote in local and general elections.
13 You can leave school.	14 You can get a full time job.
15 You can sign a deed poll to change your name.	16 You can marry with the consent of your parent or guardian.
17 You can be prescribed contraception with your parents' consent.	18 You can buy cigarettes, tobacco, liqueur chocolates and fireworks.
19 You can sit on a Jury.	20 You can join the Police Force.
21 You can claim unfair dismissal from work.	22 You can give blood.
23 You can adopt a child.	24 You can stand for local council or Parliament.
25 You can buy something on hire purchase (HP).	26 You can pawn an article in a pawnshop.
27 You can buy a pet animal.	28 Girls can consent to sex.

INFORMATION SHEET 4a

GROWING UP IN THE COMMUNITY

Initiation – Christianity

Initiation is a ritual that someone goes through to become a member of some group. In British society you simply grow up, although many clubs and other groups have special ceremonies to show that someone has become a full member. Guides and Scouts make a promise in front of the whole company or troop and the armed forces have special graduation ceremonies. In religions there are often very elaborate ceremonies, or rites, to help a young person understand the commitment that they are taking on and to give the faith community a chance to support them.

Sarah had been going to her local Church of England for several years. She had outgrown the Sunday School and had been challenged by a teacher to think about her faith more deeply. Recently there had been a group of young Christians in school talking about the importance of making a public stand for your faith. She decided that it was time to remake the vows that her parents and godparents had made at her baptism – but this time for herself.

She had a long chat with her parents and with her vicar and they all felt that it was right for her to be confirmed. Classes had just started in the church and so she went along so that she could learn more about the commitment that she was about to make. Every day she tried to read a short passage in her Bible and to think about what it meant to her.

On the big Sunday itself she was very nervous, but there were twelve other people being confirmed along with her. She wore a white dress, although not many girls did these days, because she wanted to symbolise the new start and purity that she wanted Christ to bring into her life. During the Communion service the Bishop asked Sarah and the other candidates the three questions that had been asked at their baptisms:
Do you turn to Christ?
Do you repent of your sins?
Do you renounce evil?
Each of the candidates replied firmly, 'I do'.

Then Sarah took her turn to kneel before the Bishop who laid his hands on her head and said 'Confirm O Lord, your servant Sarah Anne, with your Holy Spirit'. He had put on his mitre (hat) for this part of the service as it is one of the symbols of his authority. Although Sarah felt no different outside, she felt a warm glow inside, that she had been able to show to those around her that she wanted to be a Christian in her own right, and that the Holy Spirit would help her to live a Christian life. The whole congregation of the church was supporting her too. It had been an important and special day after lots of learning and preparation. She was also now able to take the bread and wine of Holy Communion and felt fully part of her church.

Two of Sarah's friends had also been interested in what the group in their school had said, but their ceremonies were in their own, different churches.

Tom had been brought up as a Roman Catholic and went to Mass each week. Since he was seven and had made his first communion, he had been able to receive the bread and wine at Mass. Now he had thought more deeply about the meaning of it all and wanted, like Sarah, to show others that this faith was important to him. He was also confirmed, after going to preparation classes, during a special Mass, by his Bishop. He chose a new name to be used just at his confirmation too – Peter, as he admired St Peter, one of the first followers of Jesus.

Anita went with her parents to the local Baptist church. She had seen many older people being baptised and now decided that she was ready to make the commitment too. Like Sarah and Tom, she went to classes to find out more about her faith. One Sunday evening she was baptised. Before she stepped in to the baptistry tank full of water, she spoke out to the whole congregation and told them about how she had thought more about her faith and wanted to publicly show her commitment to Christ. This was her testimony. She then walked down the five steps into the warm water and listened as her minister asked her if she was willing to live the Christian life. When she replied that she was, he said, 'Anita, on your profession of faith, I gladly baptise you in the name of the Father, the Son and the Holy Spirit'. He leant her back totally under the water for a second. When she came up again she walked out of the baptistry by steps on the other side, showing that she had left her old life and started a new one. The congregation sang a hymn and welcomed her as a full member.

INFORMATION SHEET 4b

GROWING UP IN THE COMMUNITY

Initiation – Hinduism and Judaism

HINDUISM

In India the sacred thread ceremony is important in the life of every teenage boy. Does it still happen in Britain? There are many different Hindu communities in Britain, each coming from a different part of India, or from Africa. Many are Gujarati, and they keep the rites faithfully. Others also keep the rites, but with some concession to Western lifestyle. The ceremony can take place at any time, but must be before the boy or man marries. Surbjit had his ceremony when he was 23. He had been born in Britain of Indian parents, and wanted to get married. So he felt that he must go through the ceremony.

A Hindu priest was invited to his parents' home to run the ceremony, and many guests, both British and Indian, were invited. It took place in the garden. The priest had taught Surbjit how to follow the Hindu way of life. He was taught how to pray, about graces and prayers before meals and how to meet people. Up to this point he had been excused such things.

During the ceremony a long, thin thread was given to him. He will wear it over his left shoulder all of the time. It may be changed once a year. The thread is in three strands, each of which stands for three main aspects of God – the Creator, Preserver and Destroyer of life. Having promised to follow the teachings of Hinduism, Surbjit was then considered an adult within the religion.

Not all Hindus will carry out this ceremony. Only certain castes do it – the Brahmins, Vaisyas and Ksatriyas. Surbjit's parents are Brahmins. Yet the customs are dying out in Britain. Surbjit will probably not have the ceremony performed for his son because he will have grown up in the British way of life.

JUDAISM

Benjamin celebrated his Bar Mitzvah the day after his thirteenth birthday – according to the Hebrew calendar, and to Jewish custom. He belongs to an Orthodox community in Britain. The Hebrew calendar is slightly different to the British one as it follows the moon, but it is usually within about a month of the British. To become Bar Mitzvah means to become a 'son of the commandment' and a full member of the Jewish religion.

Beforehand he had to learn from the Rabbi at the synagogue what it meant to be a Jew. He learned to read Hebrew, although he had already begun this at *shul* (Hebrew classes after normal school time), as the scriptures are written in Hebrew. He was taught how to pray and how to wear *tallit* (a prayer shawl) and *tephilin* (small black boxes containing part of the Hebrew scripture worn on the arm and forehead) for weekday prayers. He also learned more about the history of his religion and what his responsibilities as an adult would be. Most important of all, he learned to read (and to understand) the passage from the Torah that he would read in the synagogue.

On the Sabbath after his birthday he was very nervous and excited. At the point in the synagogue service where the reading of the Torah took place, Benjamin was called up to read the Hebrew scripture aloud. He chanted it as he had been taught and used a special silver pointer to follow the words. His father stood by proudly, with the Rabbi, and helped him with a difficult bit. Then, after the service, there was a celebration for the whole congregation, and later a big family party. He was given presents and speeches were made. From now on he would be treated as an adult in the religion, and would count as one of the *minyan* – the minimum number of ten men needed for a service to take place.

In Orthodox Judaism girls do not become Bat Mitzvah (daughter of the commandment) in the synagogue as women play no part in worship.

However, when Deborah, Benjamin's sister, had been in Year 8 at school the previous year, the family had spent a year in Israel and her whole class had had a special celebration and party for the girls. Girls become Bat Mitzvah at the age of 12. In a Reform community girls have the same ceremony as boys.

INFORMATION SHEET 4c

GROWING UP IN THE COMMUNITY
Initiation – Sikhism, Buddhism and Islam

SIKHISM

Fourteen year old Ranjit recently decided that he was ready to become a full member of the Sikh *Khalsa*, or community of Sikhs. If he had been living in a big city with lots of Sikhs around, then he would have been able to go to classes which had been organised and advertised, but as he lives in an area with comparatively few Sikhs, he went to the khalsa at his gurdwara and explained that he felt he would like to be fully initiated into the Sikh religion.

There were three other people who also wanted to be baptised. One girl was Ranjit's age and the other two were a couple in their forties. This is not unusual as Sikhs can have this ceremony at any age when they feel ready for it, as long as they can read the prayers and observe the five Ks. Some may repeat the ceremony if they have lapsed. The small group met together for preparation classes so that they really understood what their faith was about and the commitment that they would be taking on. After their initiation, they would be expected to observe certain rules: to pray daily before sunrise, at sunset and when going to bed; to wear the five Ks; not to drink alcohol or smoke; to be faithful in marriage.

Before the ceremony the four of them washed and put on the five Ks which they would then wear for life. These are: long hair (*Kesh*), baggy shorts (*Kacchera*), a steel bangle (*Kara*), a comb (*Kangha*) and a curved sword (*Kirpan*). Five members of the *Khalsa* – representing the *panj pyares* – lead the ceremony and asked the novices to make vows dedicating themselves to the teachings of Sikhism and the love of God and other people. Prayers were said, and there was a reading from the Guru Granth Sahib, the Holy Book. Then sugar crystals were mixed with water in a steel bowl and stirred with a two-edged dagger. This liquid, called *amrit*, was given to the novices to drink and put on their eyes and head. Each happened five times. The ceremony ended with the sharing of *prashad*, special food, which is usual at all Sikh services.

Following their Amrit, or baptism, Ranjit and his friends were regarded as full members of the Khalsa. They also took on new names. Ranjit took on the surname *Singh* (meaning lion) and the women became *Kaur* (meaning princess). This is to show equality within the religion.

BUDDHISM

Hannah had been following the teachings of the Buddha for some time and was a keen supporter of the local group of Friends of the Western Buddhist Order. Now that she was 30, she decided that she must make some big decisions in her life, and one of them was to become an ordained Buddhist. Buddhism is a way of life, with practical guidelines about how to live, rather than a fully organised religion, with lots of rituals. So her 'Going to refuge' was a simple ceremony at which she repeated three times before the leader of her local Buddhist community, 'I go for refuge to the Buddha' (the founder of Buddhism), 'I go for refuge to the Dharma' (the teachings of the Buddha), 'I go for refuge to the Sangha' (the community of Buddhists). She then repeated the five precepts, or moral guidelines of Buddhists. Hannah also chose to be known by a new, eastern name, to mark out her new start in life. She would continue her work as a social worker, but she had now publicly shown her following of Buddhism.

ISLAM

Tariq, the youngest in his family, had been 12 last birthday and now that the Muslim month of Ramadan was about to start, he knew that he must now fast (not eat) during daylight hours like the rest of his family. This was the only difference that his age meant to his religion. Unlike other religions, there is no ceremony to mark the personal commitment of the believer. Muslims are expected to follow the five pillars of Islam as an obligation anyway. For Tariq this meant that every day he was used to reciting the *Shahadah*, or creed, of Islam. He prayed five times a day and gave part of his money to the poor. He would now join in the annual fast during Ramadan, and hoped one day to be able to go on a special pilgrimage to Mecca, the most holy city for Muslims.

WORKSHEET 4

GROWING UP IN THE COMMUNITY

Initiation

Look at the accounts of initiation ceremonies in different religions. Your teacher might also have some videos or extra books to give you more information. They all concentrate on becoming a member of a religion in Britain today.

1. On your own or in a group write a play in which a group of friends discuss their own different religious initiation ceremonies.

2. Find someone who has been through one of these ceremonies to come and talk to you about it, and to answer your questions.

3. In pairs list all of the things that are similar in the ceremonies. Are there certain things that happen in most?

4. Imagine that you have been through one of these ceremonies. (You may really have been). Write a letter to a friend saying what happened, why, and how you felt about it.

5. Discuss:
   - How can religious communities help their young people as they grow up?
   - Is there any value in initiation ceremonies? If so, what is it? If not, why not?

6. In Britain there is no ceremony to show that young people have legally come of age and are full members of society. Using all that you have learned from this work, make up your own ceremony for young people as they come of age in Britain. Present it appropriately. Try to include an aspect of each of these things:

   - Place
   - People present
   - Leader(s)
   - Clothes
   - Tests
   - Words/vows
   - Actions
   - Symbols
   - Religious part
   - Readings
   - Preparation

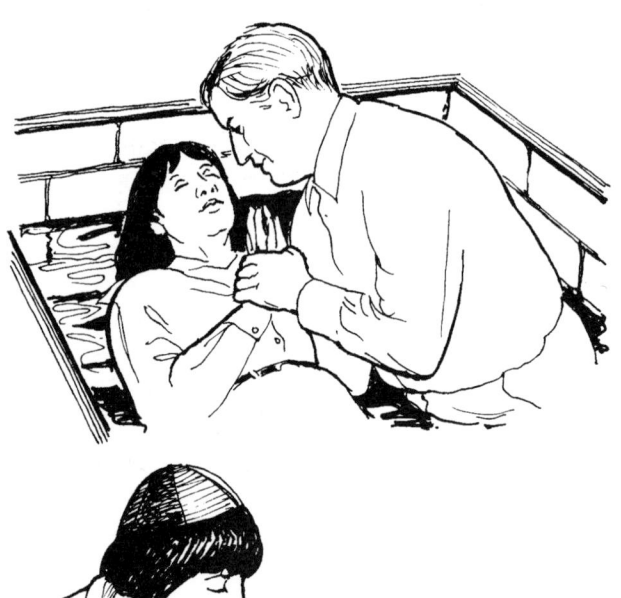

WORKSHEET 5

GROWING UP IN THE COMMUNITY

Rules

Get into small groups of about four or five people. You are going to role play one or more of the following situations.

Role play means that you take on the role of someone else and try to behave and speak as if you were in their particular situation. You need to forget about yourself and what you believe, and try to think yourself into someone else's shoes.

SURVIVAL

You are a group of school students on a trip to Europe.

The plane that you are on crashes in very poor weather conditions. All other passengers and crew are killed. You are the only survivors.

The area where you have crashed is heavily forested. There is a small stream nearby. The plane is badly damaged and there is a lot of wreckage strewn around. You have no idea where the nearest settlement is, or even where you are.

You do not know how long it will take for you to be rescued.

Make a list of the rules that you will need to make and keep if you are to survive until help arrives.

NEW TOWN

You are the town council of a new town that has been built in the countryside around _____.

It is a smart and modern town with all modern amenities.

There are no laws and rules for this town.

You must draw up a list of bye-laws which you think will be needed if the new town is to flourish and everyone who lives there is to be happy.

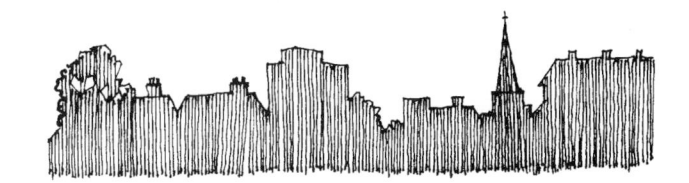

NEW BUSINESS

You are the managing directors of a new business which has just been set up.

Your company will manufacture and sell wooden toys.

You have no staff yet and only a building to work from.

You must draw up a list of the rules that you will need for the company to do well.

NEW RELIGIOUS GROUP

You are the elders of a new religious group which has set up in the area.

You have a brand new building to meet in, which could be let out to other people to raise money to run on. You have a small but faithful number of people in your group. Some are families.

You must draw up a list of rules that your organisation will need if you are to flourish.

INFORMATION SHEET 5

GROWING UP IN THE COMMUNITY

Rules

Wherever two or more people meet together there tend to be rules. They may have the status of laws, or they may be informal arrangements between people – unwritten rules. You soon know if you have broken them because other people let you know. If you did the role plays on worksheet 5, what sort of rules did you come up with for your survival or your organisations? Did you have lots of detailed rules, or just a few that covered everything? Did everyone agree with the rules?

We need rules in society to prevent chaos from happening. If there were no traffic laws then car drivers would soon bump into each other going whichever way they fancied on a roundabout, and if there were no laws which said that you should not steal, people would take what they wanted from shops and shopkeepers could no longer earn a living. If there were no rules in football then there would be no pleasure in winning as you could cheat as much as you liked, and no one would know what was going on. If there were no rules preventing people from walking on railway lines then there would be more accidents, and so on.

Many organisations have rules, as the role plays showed. Businesses have rules about health and safety on the premises, their product, and their policy on various issues. Youth organisations have rules about who may be a member, how to behave and how they are run. Religions have rules about their organisation (e.g. who may be a priest and how to train, looking after buildings etc.) and about the behaviour of followers. In all cases these rules safeguard those involved and also help to unite them by showing that they follow a common set of guidelines.

It is often good to have rules in a family or group of people who live together. It means that everyone knows where they stand, and it gives the family a chance to get on together – provided that the rules are fair in the first place, that everyone understands them and understands why they were set up. Understanding why we have rules is important. Some rules may seem stupid at first sight. 'Why shouldn't I walk across the grass?' or 'Why should I have to wear a school uniform?' We need to look behind the rule to the reason – in the above cases, because someone has spent a long time making the grass look attractive, or you will take mud etc. into a building; because wearing a uniform means that everyone can be equal.

Rules are good, then, because they can guide people about how to live or behave in certain circumstances, and they can protect the freedom of individuals from others. Yet there is also a danger that they can mean loss of freedom if they are too prescriptive, and that can lead to people keeping laws or rules just for the sake of it, and not because of the underlying reasons, which are often far more important. Religions believe that there are rules, or order, in the natural world, and that God put order there to prevent chaos in the world around us.

INFORMATION SHEET 6

GROWING UP IN THE COMMUNITY

Religious Rules

All religions have rules which their followers are expected to keep. For some there are a lot of detailed rules, for others there are simply main guidelines. In almost all cases the rules will be found in the holy book of each religion, and go back to the foundation of the religion. Some were given by the founder, others are interpretations of his teachings. Often there are the main rules for each religion and then other rules which may not be so authoritative or there may be different extra rules for different denominations. One of the reasons for preparing young people for their initiation is to help them to learn these rules, and the reasons behind them, so that they are better able to live out their religion.

For **Jews**, the Ten Commandments are the key to their religion. These laws were given by God to Moses for the Jewish people on their way to the land he had promised them, about 3500 years ago. If the Jews kept these laws then they would be able to live a good life in their new land. The Ten Commandments cover all aspects of life, but they are quite general. So over the years Jewish scholars interpreted the laws for each situation. The Ten Commandments are found in the Torah (which means 'law') and this book (the first five books of the Old Testament) is the most authoritative Jewish scripture. The rest of the Old Testament (called the Tenach) is also important, along with the Talmud which is an interpretation of it.

Christians also accept the Ten Commandments, but they believe that Jesus added to them by saying that what was far more important than keeping laws, was to love God and other people. If you do that, you will then keep all of the laws! His teaching is found in the New Testament, and Christians accept the whole Bible as authoritative. Some denominations teach that only the Bible is needed to guide a Christian in life, others say that the teachings of the Church are equally important, and Roman Catholics especially accept the authority of the Pope.

A **Muslim** is literally anyone who submits to the will of Allah. The teachings of Islam were revealed to Muhammed, the final prophet of Islam, by Allah, and are to be found in the Qur'an. The five general teachings of Islam are known as the Five Pillars of Faith. *Shahadah* means 'declaring faith in Allah', and Muslims must recite their creed every day. They will also pray five times a day – *salat* – and during the month of Ramadan they will fast during daylight hours to discipline themselves – *saum*. *Zakat* is giving to others, and every Muslim must give a share of their wealth each year to those less fortunate. Finally most Muslims try to make the *Hajj*, or pilgrimage to Mecca at least once in their lifetime.

Buddhists do not believe in a God, but they follow the practical teachings of the Buddha who lived about 2500 years ago in India. The main aim of Buddhism is to overcome the sufferings of this life which are caused by human hatred, greed and ignorance, and to move towards a state of peace called Nirvana. The Buddha taught that to escape from the cycle of craving and suffering in life, one must follow the Middle Way. This has eight steps and is a practical way to overcome suffering, based on morality, (basic principles to guide action), meditation (freeing the mind) and wisdom (understanding what life is like). Buddhist teaching is aimed at respect for all living things.

Briefly, **Hindus** have no set rules as such, but follow certain guidelines. The main one of these is dharma, or right conduct/duty. In doing this, Hindus practise *ahisma*, harmlessness, and they seek the truth.

Sikhs also have no set moral rules, but they follow the teachings of the Ten Gurus who led the religion from its founding about 450 years ago and the Guru Granth Sahib, which is now the authority of the religion and contains the teaching of the Ten Gurus. They basically try to love God and people, to treat all people equally and to defend and support the Sikh way of life.

WORKSHEET 6

GROWING UP IN THE COMMUNITY

Religious Rules

1 Copy out and complete these paragraphs.

All religions have rules or guidelines. They are usually based on the _____ of their founder, and can be found in their _____ _____. During their preparation for _____ young people are often taught the rules of their faith.

The _____ _____ are the most important rules for Jews, and these can be found in the _____. Jews also follow the teachings found in the _____ and the _____. Christians also accept the Ten Commandments, but for them the teachings of _____ emphasise _____ for God and others. If they do that then they will keep any rules that are made.

Muslims must submit to the will of _____. There are five main things which a Muslim must do. These are: to recite the _____ daily; to pray _____ times a day; to give to charity, to _____ during Ramadan; and to try to go on pilgrimage _____ in their lifetime. Buddhists follow the practical teachings of the Buddha, which include _____ steps following the Middle Way to right life. Hindus and Sikhs have no set rules, but Hindus try to practise _____ and to seek _____; while Sikhs aim to be just to all _____.

2 In most religions there are rules that affect the daily lives of followers. Most would say that these rules are not restrictive, but they gladly keep them as they are reminders of their faith in their God.
a) Find out more about the rules of one religion and the way that they affect the daily life of followers.
b) Imagine that you have a follower of that faith coming to stay with you for a weekend. Write a list of preparations that you will need to make, and a programme for the weekend which will make allowance for the religious needs of your guest. You might think about the sort of food that you will be able to serve, things that you might do together, what you will need to provide.

3 Discuss in groups what you think are the advantages and disadvantages of religions that have strict rules for their followers? Would it be better to have no rules at all?

INFORMATION SHEET 7

GROWING UP IN THE COMMUNITY

Rules Gone Mad

Sometimes rules can do more harm than good. They can be taken to extremes and so defeat whatever point they were set up to achieve. The same can be true of unwritten rules. They can become conventions – how often do you hear people say 'But we've always done it that way, we mustn't change it'.

By the time of Jesus the Jewish teachers had expanded the Ten Commandments and added 613 laws to make clear exactly what the Ten Commandments meant. There were very explicit laws about what could and could not be done on the Sabbath e.g. harvesting wheat in any form was banned. Jesus tried to help the people to put the 'delight' back into the Sabbath by showing that it was the reason for the law that was more important. He was concerned that men should not make rules which would spoil things for others.

It is also possible for people to use the Law to support something that they are doing which is perhaps not morally right. In another story of Jesus two men passed by an injured fellow man and ignored him. They had very good excuses – they both worked in the Temple and if they stopped to help a man who was dead (for so it appeared to them) they would not be allowed to continue their work without a full ritual cleansing. You can read the story in Luke 10:25-37. Later on in the New Testament St Paul tried to explain to the early Christians that God wanted people to follow him by loving others and not just by keeping a lot of laws. Keeping laws would not get them into heaven!

There are times when it is very difficult for some people to keep a law or rule. It may be that keeping it would put them, or someone important to them, in danger; or it may be that the law conflicts with their personal beliefs. Dietrich Bonhoeffer was a German pastor during the Second World War. He taught that it was wrong for Christians to fight, and he also believed that Hitler was very wrong. So Bonhoeffer joined in the plot to assassinate him. He was arrested and, in 1945, executed for treason. For him, State laws conflicted with moral laws and he had to decide which to follow. He used his conscience, and what he believed was ultimately right in God's eyes, to make his choice.

This leads us to see that there also exist moral laws which are not written laws, but codes of behaviour and practice which are accepted in society. These moral laws sometimes change over the years with society. Older people might say 'that was never accepted in my day'. For young people growing up and developing their own codes of beliefs and morals, it can sometimes be very difficult to know which way to turn.

Looking at this issue in a totally different way today, the idea of conventions (see Wordlist) can cause problems. The saying 'blue for a boy and pink for a girl' has become rooted in our society and sexual stereotypes can become 'rules gone mad'. (The accepted norm is that boys play with train sets and girls with dolls, boys help Dad with the car and girls help Mum in the kitchen.) To break this convention can lead to prejudice and opposition. Boys who prefer to cook or sew are teased and girls who like messing about with cars are labelled as 'tomboys'. Sometimes, however, it is good for people to take the plunge and step outside of these conventions, to challenge people about what really lies behind their thinking.

Copyright © 1996 by Sally Lynch. The Publishers grant permission for multiple copies of this page to be made for use solely within that institution.

WORKSHEET 7

GROWING UP IN THE COMMUNITY

Rules Gone Mad

1. Think about your school rules. a) Are there too many, or too few? b) What are the reasons for each? c) Would you change them in any way?

2. Look up the story of Jesus and his disciples on the Sabbath – Mark 2:23-28 in pairs. One of you take the role of the Pharisees, and the other take the role of Jesus and the disciples. Try to explain to each other why you have taken your particular stance over this issue.

3. Look up the story of the Good Samaritan in Luke 10:25-37. Can you think of any situations today where people might use the Law or rules as backing for not doing something which they ought to. [The TV programme *That's Life* used to run a slot: 'it's more than my job's worth'. Can you think of any examples of this? The one opposite should start you off].

4. Can you think of any times when a person might feel that they have to break a law? Try to give some secular and religious examples.

5. St Paul wrote:
   'Everyone must submit himself to the governing authorities, for there is no authority except that which God has established . . .' (Romans 13:1).
   a) Do you agree with this?
   b) Can you think of times when it might cause problems for a Christian?
   c) You might like to look up the rest of the passage too.

6. Find out more about Dietrich Bonhoeffer and discuss whether you agree with what he did. Can you find any other examples of such action?

7. Consider the sexual stereotypes and conventions in our society.
   a) List things that are associated only with boys, and those associated only with girls.
   b) Would you want to change these conventions? Why/why not?

8. Think about the idea of moral rules. In what ways have codes of morals changed over the years with regard to: clothes and appearance; sexual behaviour; lifestyles?

Copyright © 1996 by Sally Lynch. The Publishers grant permission for multiple copies of this page to be made for use solely within that institution.

INFORMATION SHEET 8a

GROWING UP IN THE COMMUNITY
Breaking Rules

If you have a party until 3 a.m. and make a lot of noise, you are breaking a social custom or law. If you are a Muslim and do not pray five times a day, you are breaking a religious law; but neither of these are crimes. Most people break moral or social laws or conventions at some time in their lives. A crime is different. A crime is an act forbidden by the law of the land and committed with a wrongful intent. That is, a person knows they are breaking the law of a country. There are many types of crimes, some more serious than others depending on whether other people are hurt or not, or affected in some way.

CAUSES

The crime rate in this country is on the increase, in particular burglary, violent crime and rape. Violence is also more often used as a way of sorting out problems or making a point. In most cases there are many reasons why a person commits a particular crime; including immediate reasons and probably longer term, underlying reasons. These general reasons can be broken down into specific causes. We might picture the causes of crime like this:

ATTITUDES

People in society have different attitudes towards crime and law breakers. The victims of each crime will naturally feel distressed and possibly want their revenge on the criminal. They may feel that very harsh punishment is due, the Old Testament idea of making 'The punishment fit the crime'.

Other people say that the offender should make some kind of retribution for what he has done; that is, to pay the victim or society, back in some way. Others say that the criminal himself needs help and that the reasons why he committed the crime need to be examined. There are also members of society who believe that it is important that offenders should be punished, but that the punishment should be 'fair' and also economical on taxpayers' money. Some of these people are involved with organisations such as NACRO and the Howard League for Penal Reform – trying to find the most suitable and effective punishments and making the whole system better. Such organisations also try to help the public to prevent and to fight crime. They also try to help us to see and to accept criminals as people who need help. This is a major task, because society tends to brand someone as a criminal long after he has served his punishment, whatever it is.

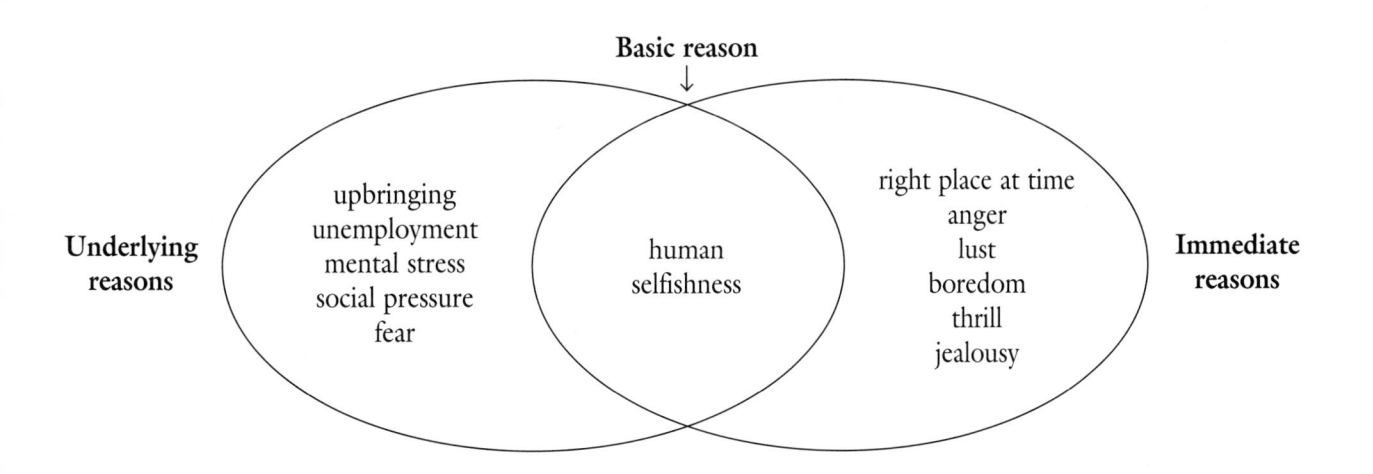

Basic reason ↓

Underlying reasons
- upbringing
- unemployment
- mental stress
- social pressure
- fear

human selfishness

Immediate reasons
- right place at time
- anger
- lust
- boredom
- thrill
- jealousy

INFORMATION SHEET 8b

GROWING UP IN THE COMMUNITY
Breaking Rules

There are a number of ways of punishing people today.

Youth Custody Centre: a prison for young people.

Attendance Centre: a centre which offenders must attend for 12 or 24 hours in two-hour sessions, usually on Saturdays (so that they can hold down a job if they have one).

Binding over: the offender pays a sum of money to the Court on the agreement that he will behave himself. If he does not, then he loses the money.

Community service order: the offender is made to work unpaid for the community for a certain length of time. If the order is broken, he may be resentenced.

Day Training Centre: attendance is ordered for up to 60 days so that the offender can receive training to help him get a job.

Disqualification: the driving licence is taken away for a length of time.

Discharge: no punishment is appropriate, the offender is let free.

Fine: a sum of money is paid to the court.

Probation order: the offender is free, but must report to a probation officer and keep certain conditions. The probation officer should help him to reform.

Prison: a person may be sentenced to a length of time in one of HM Prisons. Here a person loses all freedom, including the power to think for himself, to decide when he will do things and so on. (This is changing a little.) The prisoner also loses: job, contact with family and friends, own clothes, choice of company etc. He will mix in with many other criminals and have only monotonous work to do, in some prisons this is still sewing mailbags. The prisoner receives a little money from this with which to buy toiletries and cigarettes. There will be a strict daily routine to follow. When the prisoner leaves, there will be a discharge grant and clothes, but that is all. Often prisoners will have lost their jobs, and will not have been paying into insurance or pension funds. They may have no home to go to, and no family to care for them. Many people say that a person's real punishment starts when they leave prison. Perhaps that is why the rate of re-offending is so high, and many offenders end up inside again.

Most religions have some punishments for people who break their own rules. In the case of Christianity it is up to the individual to make their peace with other people and with God. In some ways their conscience will punish them. Some churches, especially the Roman Catholic Church, have a sacrament called Reconciliation, where a person talks through their 'sin' with a priest, and may be given something positive to do to make amends. In extreme cases some religions try to enforce punishments on those who have offended them. For example an English author, Salman Rushdie, wrote a book called *The Satanic Verses* which Muslims claimed was a blasphemy against Allah. The world Muslim leader has declared a death penalty on Rushdie and he has gone into hiding.

WORKSHEET 8

GROWING UP IN THE COMMUNITY

Breaking Rules

1. a) On your own write down on a slip of paper one law or school rule or convention that you would really like to break. Fold up your paper and give it in. One of the class should mix up the papers and then give them out randomly to the class. Take it in turns to read out the rule, law or convention on the paper that you now have. You might guess who wrote it!
   b) Sort out the papers into piles of similar laws or rules.
   (i) Which are the most popular ones to be broken?
   (ii) Why do you think this is?
   (iii) Ask each other why you wrote down what you did.
   (iv) Can this tell you anything about why people break school rules, or, more importantly, why people break laws?

2. a) Look through some newspapers and cut out examples of broken laws.
   b) In small groups, take one example each and read it carefully.
   (i) Discuss why you think the person or people broke the law.
   (ii) Is there more than one reason?
   c) Share your findings with other groups in the class.
   (i) Does any pattern emerge about why people break laws?
   (ii) What sort of laws are most commonly broken?

3. a) Invite a Roman Catholic priest into your school to talk about Reconciliation.
   Do you agree that it is helpful to 'confess' sins to a priest?
   b) Discuss:
   If we have punishments for certain crimes by law in Britain, should religions have punishments for certain things? There were many in the Old Testament (see, for example Exodus 21:12-27), why do you think that Jews and Christians do not use these today?

4. a) What do you think could be done to prevent crime?
   b) Write an article or design a poster which helps the public to cut down crime.

5. Do you think that the churches or religious groups could do anything about rising crime figures and criminals themselves? If so, what and how might they go about it?

6. Find out more about the work of NACRO or the Howard League for Penal Reform. Do you think that their work is valuable? Give reasons for your answers.

Neighbourhood Watch scheme growing

Woman arrested for shoplifting

BOY OF 13 ACCUSED OF MURDER

Copyright © 1996 by Sally Lynch. The Publishers grant permission for multiple copies of this page to be made for use solely within that institution.

INFORMATION SHEET 9a

GROWING UP IN THE COMMUNITY
Punishment

There are four main reasons why people are punished, and often the actual punishment given is for a combination of these reasons. Different people see some reasons as more important than others.

PROTECTION

Society often needs to be protected from the offenders' actions, and they also may need to be protected from themselves. The most obvious type of punishment to achieve this is imprisonment. In the Bible people were imprisoned if they were thought to be a danger to society, e.g. Barabbas and Paul, for different reasons.

RETRIBUTION/REVENGE

This is probably the oldest purpose of punishment and it is the idea of 'getting your own back' on someone. If a person has committed a crime then their punishment should be fitting. This is supported in the Old Testament as 'An eye for an eye' etc. (Exodus 21:23-24). The danger with this purpose alone is that it may become a personal retaliation and hitting back, with both sides continuing a running battle. It can be very negative. Jesus teaches against this in the New Testament and forbids the taking of revenge (Matthew 5:38-47). The most obvious type of punishment here was the death penalty for murder – 'life for life'.

REFORM

Many people prefer this purpose as it is more positive and helps both the offender and society. It is the idea that the person who has committed the crime needs help and they receive this in various ways so that they will not offend again. This is quite expensive in time, money and people. Some punishments might include Detention Centres and Community service.

DETERRENCE

This is the idea that someone is punished to put themselves or others off committing crimes. If others see what has happened to an offender, hopefully they will decide that they do not want that to happen to them and so they will not offend. The offender will hopefully not wish to suffer in that way again. The punishment must therefore be severe enough without being unfair. Examples might include fines or the death penalty, depending on the crime.

Some people suggest another reason for punishing people and that is simply to ensure that the law is upheld (kept) this is called **vindication**.

INFORMATION SHEET 9b

GROWING UP IN THE COMMUNITY

Punishment

LIFE IN PRISON

Most people will talk about prison when they think of people being punished for committing crimes. Although there is a wide range of alternative punishments in Britain, prison is still one of the most common. Some people suggest that it is too easy to send offenders to prison and that other options should be tried first. These might be more positive and help the offender to see the wrong that has been done, and to reform. Community service might be an example. Such people say that the offender will just learn more from other inmates in the prison and come out worse than before. Other people say that what young people in particular need is a 'short sharp shock' and that prison will teach them a lesson. The debate will continue for a long time.

It costs £494 per week, on average, to keep a person in prison in Britain. You might like to consider how this is spent. Many people are in prison while they are waiting for their case to come up in court and to be sentenced. These people are on remand. On 1 March 1993, there were 42,870 prisoners held in 128 prisons in England and Wales, served by 38,233 staff.

The media sometimes distorts our picture of prison life. Some parts of the media suggest that our prisons are too overcrowded and places where violence and crime flourish; other areas of the media say that with the number of new and modern prisons growing, offenders have better leisure facilities than the public and that life is like a holiday camp. Television has a tendency to glamorise the prison system, or to make it slightly unreal. People's opinions are swayed by one or more of these influences. What we all tend to forget is the one thing that is common to all prisoners – they have lost their freedom.

On arrival at a woman's prison, Michelle saw a notice that all inmates see on the wall: 'Her Majesty's Prison Service serves the public by keeping in custody those committed by the courts. Their duty is to look after them with humanity and help them to lead law abiding and useful lives after release'. Michelle hoped that her release would be before the two years she had been given for the shoplifting that she now regretted.

As the gates and doors clanged shut behind her, all of her belongings were taken away and listed, ready for her release. She was seen by the doctor and then shown to her small cell which had only a bed, table, small cupboard, chair and no curtains at the high-up windows. The door was locked and she was alone with her thoughts and the few posessions that she had been allowed to keep – her watch, wedding ring and two pairs of earrings; a walkman, flask and mug and a few pencils, plus a few other bits and pieces and six photographs of her children. She would only be allowed one letter to them each week, and one short visit from her parents each fortnight.

Over the next few weeks she got used to the strict prison regime, being allowed out of her cell at 8 a.m. for breakfast, working until lunch at 12 p.m. and again in the afternoon. She had half an hour's exercise each day and two hours association time with other prisoners, but every night they were locked up at 8 p.m. At weekends they were usually in their cells for even longer. Michelle was given work in the laundry and paid £6.50 per week, but she never handled any money – it was put on an account which she spent in the canteen shop on soap and sweets, and stamps to write an extra letter each week to her children. There were opportunites for her to study for the GCSEs that she had never bothered about at school, but most of all she hated the fact that her every movement was monitored. She couldn't even decide for herself when she wanted to go to the toilet.

WORKSHEET 9

GROWING UP IN THE COMMUNITY

Punishment

1. Look at each of the five purposes of punishment on Information Sheet 9a and at these quotations. Match up the quotation to the correct purpose of punishment to see what each of these people believe is important.

   My object all sublime
   I shall achieve in time
   To make the punishment fit the crime
   The punishment fit the crime

   The Mikado (a Japanese Judge)
   Gilbert and Sullivan

   Crimson with fury, Oliver started up; overthrew the chair and table, seized Noah by the throat . . . they dragged Oliver into the dust cellar, and there locked him up. 'Oh! Charlotte' said Mrs Sowerberry, 'what a mercy we have not all been murdered in our beds'.

   Oliver Twist
   Charles Dickens

   . . . they saw Aslan and Edmund walking together in the dewy grass. . . There is no need to tell you what Aslan was saying, but it was a conversation which Edmund never forgot. 'Here is your brother' he said, 'and there is no need to talk to him about what is past'.

   The Lion, the Witch and the Wardrobe
   C. S. Lewis

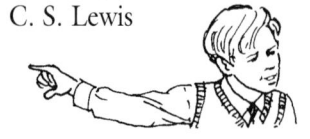

   The object of punishment is prevention from evil.

   Lectures and Reports on Education (1854)
   Horace Mann

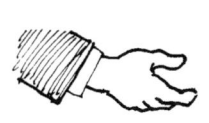

2. Draw a picture or find some examples of pictures which show each purpose of punishment in action.

3. Think about each purpose of punishment and discuss these questions:

PROTECTION	REVENGE
• Who needs to be protected? • How can we best protect society? • Is prison the best protection?	• Is revenge always bad? • What sorts of punishment are about revenge? • Who gets their revenge?
DETERRENCE	**REFORM**
• Why is this important? • How is it used in schools? • Is it right to make examples of people?	• What does this really mean • Is it really possible? • Why do many people think this is best?

4. In 1986 a London vicarage was broken into. The vicar and another man were beaten up, and his daughter was raped. On television the vicar said that he forgave the men. Yet when sentences were passed on them he said that they were too lenient. What do you think?

5. a) Find out more about what attitudes different people have towards this issue. Invite a panel of people in to school for a 'Question Time' about punishment. You might include a priest, doctor, school governor, JP and so on. Each of you write questions that you would like to ask the panel. Have a chairperson and make it a formal session.

   b) Write up the Question Time as a newspaper report or simple account.

6. What are your own feelings about punishment? Write them as a memo to yourself or in pairs carefully explain your views to each other (without interrupting or disagreeing).

7. a) Do you think that being religious makes a difference to people's views about punishment? Discuss this in groups.

   b) Find out what the words justice and accountability mean. Do these words mean more to religious people when they think about a God who created this world and the people in it? Discuss. Produce a poster which shows why one religious group believe punishment is important.

INFORMATION SHEET 10

GROWING UP IN THE COMMUNITY

Capital Punishment

Some time ago during a radio phone-in programme on the theme of punishment, a man rang in to say that he had sat on a jury which found a woman guilty of murder. Her name was Ruth Ellis. She was the last woman to be hung in Britain. The caller said that he found his Jury Service very difficult. When the jury went out to decide on their verdict it was not easy. It seemed fairly clear that the woman was guilty, 'But', he said 'we all knew that if we found her guilty we would be passing the death sentence'.

Capital punishment is one of the oldest types of punishment, and has taken many different forms. In Britain the method was by hanging. In 1965 the British government abolished the death penalty for an experimental period. This became permanent in 1970, although it still exists for treason and piracy on the high seas. In some states of the USA capital punishment, usually by electric chair, is still used.

There are many arguments for and against the return of the death penalty. There have been at least three bills proposing its return through Parliament, but each has been defeated. The matter was considered so important that when it was debated by the governing body of the Church of England, the General Synod, in 1983, the debate was televised. It was a heated debate, but in the end Synod voted that capital punishment was wrong.

Christians are divided over this issue, although many cite Jesus' teaching about forgiveness and reform as being most important (see Matthew 5:38-48). Others are more concerned to see justice done and compassion for the victim.

Judaism does permit capital punishment, but under very strict guidelines. There should have been warnings, witnesses to the crime, and it should be carried out humanely. It is important to emphasise that the Old Testament teaching about an eye for an eye actually limits the punishment – it should not exceed the crime.

Muslims have strict rules of behaviour in the Qur'an, and the death penalty is allowed in certain, exceptional, circumstances. For some Muslims this is a way of emphasising their code of conduct and a deterrent to criminals.

It is possible for **Hindus** to put people to death according to their laws, particularly as self-defence for society. **Buddhists**, however, do not approve of capital punishment and are concerned to show compassion for all involved.

Whatever a person's religious or secular beliefs, with increasing crime and violence in the world, this issue will not go away, and young people growing up into society need to consider it for themselves.

WORKSHEET 10

GROWING UP IN THE COMMUNITY

Capital Punishment

1a) Find out more about what different religions have to say about this issue and present your findings as a chart.

b) Do any religions have just one viewpoint? Why do you think many religions are divided among themselves on this issue? Which would you agree with most? Why?

2 Look at this newspaper article and then discuss it in groups.

3a) Work in pairs. One of you list all of the arguments that you can think of FOR capital punishment. The other list all of the arguments AGAINST it. (You might not agree with all that you write.)

b) Now use your arguments against each other. Try to bring in some of the points that religious people might make.

4 Hold a class debate on the statement:
This house believes that the death penalty should be brought back for murderers in Britain today.

When 'life' hardly seems enough

YESTERDAY, George Stephenson was found guilty of the murder of four members of the Cleaver household, whom he burned alive, and of the rape of Wendy Cleaver, whom his accomplice strangled.

For this spine-chilling rampage of cruelty and hate he was sentenced to life imprisonment, with a recommendation that he should serve a minimum of 25 years. His own girlfriend felt that life was too good for him, and that he should die for this horrible crime. She is not the only one to think so.

After a week, during which we have had violent street crimes and in which an IRA terrorist responsible for killing perhaps 90 people has been jailed, many are wondering if imprisonment is sufficient punishment for criminals who so callously send others to their deaths.

These events must surely induce even those MPs who have long set their faces against capital punishment to pause and think carefully before the next vote is taken in Parliament on this emotive question.

Daily Mail

Section B

WORKING IN THE COMMUNITY

NOTES FOR THE TEACHER

AIMS AND OBJECTIVES

Aims:
- to enable students to consider the world of work, and their place in it;
- to use work experience where possible to tie in with this unit;
- to consider all aspects of work, leisure and wealth also, as leading to a balanced person.

Objectives:
Knowledge of:
- teachings and principles of the world faiths concerning work;
- religious, legal and technical aspects of wealth and leisure;
- examples of work in society.

Understanding of:
- key concepts of work, leisure and wealth;
- the need for work, wealth and leisure;
- the value of work;
- the need for balance between work and leisure.

Ability to:
- think out own plan in terms of work and a balanced life;
- consider the balance of own life, so far;
- relate the religious teachings and principles studied to work related issues;
- formulate and express an opinion clearly;
- reflect on important issues;
- research issues and report back clearly;
- relate issues discussed to local examples.

Experience of:*
- work experience;
- meeting with people at work;

* depending upon school.

CONTENTS

Wordlist
1. Work and Me
   Worksheet 1a: personal attitudes
   Worksheet 1b: research for work experience
2. What is Work?
   Worksheet 2: tasks
   Information Sheet 2a: types, attitudes
   Information Sheet 2b: reasons
3. Work in the Community
   Information Sheet 3a: electronic designer/technical assembler
   Information Sheet 3b: pharmacist
   Information Sheet 3c: classroom assistant
   Information Sheet 3d: undertaker
   Information Sheet 3e: policeman
   Information Sheet 3f: medical counsellor
   Information Sheet 3g: shop worker
   Information Sheet 3h: chartered accountant
   Worksheet 3: comparisons and discussion of above
4. Vocation and Talent
   Information Sheet 4: examples
   Worksheet 4: personal challenge/research
5. People at Work
   Worksheet 5: role plays
   Information Sheet 5: religious teachings
6. Money
   Information Sheet 6: collage of aspects
   Worksheet 6: tasks
7. Religions and Wealth
   Information Sheet 7: teachings/stories from world faiths
   Worksheet 7: tasks
8. Leisure
   Information Sheet 8: what is leisure?
   Worksheet 8: personal reflection, charity
9. Religions and Leisure
   Information Sheet 9: holy days in Great Britain
   Worksheet 9: research and debate

Copyright © 1996 by Sally Lynch. The Publishers grant permission for multiple copies of this page to be made for use solely within that institution.

Information Sheet 9: information for debate on Sunday Trading
10 A Balanced Life
Information Sheet 10: Drawing together, need for balance
Worksheet 10: produce a leaflet for school leavers based on this unit

THE SHEETS

The whole of this unit is designed to help students to consider the world of work and what their place in it will be. It is deliberately aimed to tie in with work experience where that is appropriate. There are a few other texts that are more expansive and might be helpful in this area. A topic folder on *Work*, CEM (0 85100 008 9) posters available too. *Work and the World*, Lion (0 7459 1267 2). For more detail of the religious teachings on this topic see *Guidelines for Life*, Hodder & Stoughton (0 340 51950 9) and *Moral Issues in Six Religions*, Heinemann (0 435 30299 X).

1 Work and Me
These two worksheets are designed to set the scene. The first is to get students to think for themselves and might be repeated at the end to see how or if their ideas have changed. No answers are given here to the question of whether religion plays a part in work – they will come later.

2 What is Work?
Again the worksheet comes first to get students thinking, but it may then need to be used in conjunction with the information sheets.

3 Work in the Community
These case studies are all real people, for whose time and help I am grateful. Their answers may not conform to the textbook versions of their religions, but this only serves to demonstrate to students the wide variety within every religion (not just Christianity). It may be that schools are able to draw on a panel of local people from a variety of religious and working backgrounds for students to go out and talk to or to be invited into school for a discussion forum. The sheets are deliberately designed to show both religious attitudes and also a variety of types of work and qualifications and training that are necessary. They might be used in conjunction with careers and PSE work. Students could take the tasks even further by producing a video of different types of work and how religions fit in. In task 3, Information Sheet 5 might also be of help.

4 Vocation and Talent
This section is designed to help students to grasp the idea of people's individual talents, and the belief of many religious believers that such talents are God-given, and should be used in his service. It also picks up the concept of vocation. The worksheet allows for a variety of work on this topic, from simple discussions at all ability levels, through to more detailed research work. It would be good to involve members of the local community here, to talk about their own use of talents or vocations. Perhaps a forum could be set up for students to ask questions to a panel, linked to the previous section. Additional resources: *Leading the Way*, books 1 and 2, M. Thompson, Hodder & Stoughton (0 340 51955 X; 0 340 52347 6); *Christians in Britain Today*, D. Cush, C. Miles and M. Stylianides, Hodder & Stoughton (0 340 51947 9). The video *Mother Teresa*, Richard Attenborough, BBC TV (1985).

5 People at Work
The information about the teachings of each religion is very basic, but more can be found in the books suggested. This could be done in two stages – role play first and then looking at it again in the light of the teachings. The roles can be cut up and given to students so that they cannot see each other's at first. Their own prejudices will come out here, and care will need to be taken over this so as not to reinforce them.

6 Money
This section aims to make the point that it is attitude which affects our use of money. In order to bring this out even more fully use might be made of Michel Quoist's 'Prayer before a five pound note' (*Prayers of Life*, M. Quoist, Gill and MacMillan, 7171 0158 4). Students might also listen to Abba's *Money, money, money* and the Beatles' *Can't buy me love*.

7 Religions and Wealth
More information about the teachings and stories from each religion may be found in the books mentioned above. A useful addition, if it is possible to locate a copy, would be to play a recording or a video clip of the song 'If I were a rich man' from *Fiddler on the Roof*, and to ask students whether it is so wrong for the hero to ask that God make him rich.

8 Leisure
There are lots of possibilities here – students could share their own leisure activities and hobbies, as could staff if they wished. It might be a means of learning more about each other. There are also lots of voluntary activities which people are often willing to come and talk about. I use a relative who is on the Board of Visitors of a prison – a vital and time consuming but unpaid job. This section might also help students to sort out their thoughts about part of their Record of Achievement. It could be a place to introduce them to school charity work or to schemes such as the Duke of

Edinburgh's award. The scope is almost endless! Worksheet task 1 could be made simpler for less able students by photocopying the circle chart from the information sheet (and enlarging it) to enable pupils to write or draw straight onto the sheet.

9 Religions and Leisure

The information in this sheet is fairly straightforward. Students will need help in producing the leaflet, but the idea is to get them to think about the way that a person's faith affects the whole of their life. Less able students may find it easier to make a tape, and working in pairs or groups will help all students. The debate slips might be used in a number of ways – as a whole to provide stimulus, or they might be given individually to students to use in argument. For more information about the '(reduced) Keep Sunday Special' campaign, contact KSS at The Jubilee Centre, 3 Hooper Street, Cambridge, CB1 2NZ.

10 A Balanced Life

This sheet aims to draw the whole unit together and to consider the idea of the balance needed in life. Students will again need help in designing the leaflet, but have often produced thoughtful results in the past. It might be appropriate here to look back at section 1 and to see whether any attitudes have changed.

WORDLIST

Working in the Community

This list will help you with the spellings and meanings of key words in this unit.

Abuse
treating something badly

Amoral
cannot be good or bad

Barter
to trade in goods rather than money

Constructive
something that has a purpose to it

Deregulation
doing away with certain rules

Income
money gained by working or other means

Kosher
foods which are acceptable for Jews to eat

Manual
a task done by hand

Meditation
to be still and think deeply about things

Mundane
boring or everyday tasks

Orthodox
keeping to traditional ideas and practices

Redundant
no longer needed

Talents
things that people are good at – also called gifts or abilities

Tithe
giving ten per cent of income to others

Sabbath
the Jewish holy day (sunset Friday – sunset Saturday)

Stewardship
making the best of money, time and talents, in the belief that they were given by God

Vocation
Feeling a special 'call' to a particular job or task

Voluntary
Doing something without being paid for it, doing it by choice

Wealth
Money and goods that people own

Zakat
Muslim practice of giving to charity

WORKSHEET 1a

WORKING IN THE COMMUNITY
Work and Me

This whole unit is designed to help you to think about the world of work. In this worksheet you will be thinking about your ideas about work and what you would ideally like your place to be in the world of work. Look through the questions below. They are designed to help you sort out your own attitudes at the outset. You could think about the questions for yourself and then write the answers down as a memo, or you could talk about them with a partner. You might like to do it again at the end of the visit to see if your ideas have changed at all.

1. What sort of work would you like to do in the future:

   manual; physical; academic; caring;

   with people; with animals; alone; with computers;

   indoors; outdoors; both; a specific job?

2. What sort of wages would you like to earn when you are employed:

   enough to live on;   enough for a few luxuries;

   enough to spare;   more than enough?

3. What sort of prospects would you like in a job:

   none – easy going;   some promotion;

   high status;   managerial;

   higher?

4. Do you really need to work?

5. What will you get out of work?

6. What will you offer a job?

7. Has work got anything to do with religion, and vice versa?

Discuss your answers to the above questions.

WORKSHEET 1b

WORKING IN THE COMMUNITY

Work and Me

WORK EXPERIENCE

This sheet is designed to start you thinking before you go out on work experience. It may be that your placement is linked to the sort of job that you would like to do in the future, or it may be something totally different, or it may just be a taster of work. Keep at the back of your mind the things that you considered in Worksheet 1a.

While you are out on work experience, try to talk to some of the people that you work with. Ask them the questions that you looked at in Worksheet 1a:
- Why did you choose to do this job?
- Are you happy with the wages (apart from most people's usual jokes and gripes about wages)?
- Are they realistic?
- What would you like to do in the future?
- Why do you bother to work?
- What do you get out of your work?
- What do you put into your work?
- Do you think that work has got anything to do with religion?

When you get back to school discuss (with other people) some of the answers you received. Are there any general answers (to the questions) that you can come up with?

Think about your own experience of your placement.

At the end of the first day write an account (or tape it, or just jot down headings) to say how you felt about it, how it differed from school, what attitudes you felt among the people you were with, your hopes for the rest of the work experience.

At the end of the whole work experience write (or tape or jot down) your final thoughts. Have they changed at all? What do you feel that you gave to the placement and what did you learn from it (in terms of skills, relationships with people, about the job. . .)? Discuss these experiences too.

Finally talk as a class about what you have all learned about work and about people from your time in the workplace. Does religion play a part here?

WORKSHEET 2

WORKING IN THE COMMUNITY

What is Work?

1. a) Which of the following do you class as work?

Bank clerk	Car mechanic	Doctor
House cleaning	Gardening	Driving
Teaching	Dentist	Lawyer
Reading	Taxidermy	Bricklaying
Farming	Childminding	Hairdressing
Accounting	Painting	Computing
Hospital visiting	Preaching	Sailing

   b) Discuss this list and decide if there are any differences in the types of work carried out.

   (i) Do people use their brains or their bodies?

   (ii) Are they paid or not?

   (iii) Might some be more enjoyable than others?

   (iv) Are some more difficult than others?

   c) Do the answers to all of these questions depend on who is doing the work?

2. a) Why do you think people need to work? Make a list of reasons (using what you have already found out).

   b) Using Information Sheets 2a and 2b you could then write a letter to a school leaver explaining why it is important for people to work. Try to include a religious viewpoint.

3. Make a list of all of the things that you do which you might call work (e.g. paper round, visit local old-folks home for Duke of Edinburgh award, homework, washing up). Try to identify the different types of work. You might be surprised at what you do before you even enter the world of employment.

4. a) For many people in Britain today paid employment is out of their reach – they are unemployed. Why do you think so many people are unemployed?

   b) Do religions care about this?

   c) What could the church in Britain in particular do about it?

   d) Are there any projects in your area which aim to help the unemployed? Could you find out more?

5. Design a poster which tries to show the different types of work that people do, and why people need to work. Try to bring out the need to work together as a community.

WORKING IN THE COMMUNITY

What is Work?

WHAT IS WORK?

There are many different activities which count as work. Work is not just paid employment, although that is an important aspect of life – at the very basic level of needing to earn money to live off. You work already by doing lessons at school – and hopefully at home too! You may also work by helping in the house – cooking and cleaning are still work. For some people visiting an elderly relative might seem like work and others work in their youth club or place of worship by taking on particular responsibilities. Arranging the flowers or running a Cadet meeting is still work. Your hobbies may seem like work too. Training in order to be fit for a football match may be hard work, although you may enjoy the end result.

So can we say that work is only something which is hard and that cannot be enjoyed? Obviously not. Work is not just what we get paid for, nor is it just hard labour. Work can be fun and rewarding. There are many types of work. What is paid employment for one person may be a relaxation for another. Many people do voluntary work, that is, they work for others in some way, but are not paid for it. Running a local charity group and organising different events or working in a shop for that group may be work, but it is not paid employment. The same is true of people who visit prisoners or do meals on wheels. Some people spend their weekends cleaning up ponds or clearing hedgerows. They do it because they want to help others and they enjoy it. There is job satisfaction.

For a number of people in Britain today there is no paid employment because they are unemployed. Such people may feel useless and rejected by society. Young people might take these feelings out on society by violent behaviour or vandalism. There is a real feeling of insecurity in unemployment – who will pay the bills and will we be able to cope with life without a regular income? Trying to no avail to find a job, and being turned down at lots of interviews can lead to a sense of uselessness and despair.

INFORMATION SHEET 2b

WORKING IN THE COMMUNITY
What is Work?

WHY WORK?

- The obvious reason is that nowadays we need to earn money to buy the things that we need to live (would the past system have been better, of being self-sufficient – growing what we need to eat and bartering with others for things they have that we would like? What would you barter for a TV set today?!).

- From what we have said about unemployment it is clear that people need to work in order to feel valued and of importance in the community – to have a role to play in making the whole thing work.

- This leads to the importance of everyone pulling together. We all need to work and to use our talents to the full if the community is going to flourish.

- However, it is not just about working for others, it is also about feeling proud of a job done well and the satisfaction of doing something good.

- Work also brings us into contact with other people and that is important. Humans on the whole need the company and fellowship of others to grow as people and to feel good – work can do this.

- Some people also work because they feel that they are called to do so. They believe that God wants them to do a particular job, or that by working they are serving him as well as other people.

- Work is also good and constructive and enables people to use their creative abilities well. It is better than being bored and thus becoming destructive.

Apart from the idea of earning money, these reasons can apply to any type of work that people do. All religions, then, would agree that work is very good because it uses a person's God-given gifts and abilities, it draws together the community upon which religions are based, and it values human beings. If, as the Book of Genesis says, people are made in the image of God, then they are very special and should be allowed the self-respect that comes with work. Whether they choose to accept it or not, for all people religion is linked to their work at this very basic level.

Copyright © 1996 by Sally Lynch. The Publishers grant permission for multiple copies of this page to be made for use solely within that institution.

INFORMATION SHEET 3a

WORKING IN THE COMMUNITY

Work in the Community – Sita and Rao

Sita and Rao are Hindus. They came to Britain from south India over twenty years ago and have two children, who are now married, who were born in this country. They celebrate their religion in their own home and by mixing with the few Hindu families around them. Because they live in a city with few Hindu families, they may travel to other English cities to worship together. Festivals and rites of passage are celebrated as they would be in India, although their children keep them a little less at home, wanting to join in with the English way of life. Yet Sita says that keeping the festivals is a discipline for children, even if they are less important these days. They still celebrate values.

Rao did a postgraduate study in engineering and worked in India until he saw a newspaper advert for electrical engineers in England.

He was offered a job by a good firm and came to England when he was about thirty. He became a senior engineer in a telecommunications firm, and worked his way through team leader, to principal electronic designer and became a department manager, in charge of 60–70 people. In this role he was able to help to produce new products such as pocket telephones and pagers. He took early retirement at 58 and is now able to spend half of his time in England, and half in India. He worked very hard to achieve his promotions and studied well to start with. He says that his religion did not affect his work at all.

Sita agrees. She says that Hinduism can be moulded to suit her convenience. She chooses not to pray every day as she is busy going to work, although she does sometimes stop for a second to pray on the way. She prays on a Saturday when there is time to do it properly, by bathing first. She is a technical assembler in a telecommunications firm. She says that the Hindu religion does not affect people's work, although there may be jobs where a sari might prove a problem. She chooses not to wear a sari for work, especially as her colleagues don't like it. She feels more comfortable in trousers and mixes in well with everyone else. They forget that she is Indian, and from a different community. She enjoys her work, and the friendship of working with other women.

INFORMATION SHEET 3b

WORKING IN THE COMMUNITY

Work in the Community – Helen

Helen belongs to a small Orthodox Jewish community. She works part time as a pharmacist. Having spent some years in both hospital and retail work, she is now a locum. That means that she fills in where she is needed. Currently she works every Wednesday at a local shop to cover for a day off for the pharmacist there. Other people might ring her up and ask her to cover a day or two. She is happy to do this, but she will not work on a Saturday, and she chooses not to work on a Friday.

The Jewish holy day, the Sabbath starts at sunset on Friday and lasts throughout Saturday. In England there are published books to tell Jews when the Sabbath officially begins. The time differs according to the time of year. In winter it is 3.30p.m., while in summer it is much later, and so many families bring the Sabbath in early. There is a special family meal to bring in the Sabbath, and then no cooking is done on the Sabbath. This means that there is a lot of preparation to do during the Friday. This is why Helen chooses not to work on Friday. She says that other Jews who do work on Fridays will do their cooking on Thursday night or get up early on Friday to do it.

Being a pharmacist means that Helen dispenses prescriptions, supervises the sale of medicines and advises the public about minor illnesses. She qualified for the job by taking a three-year degree course at university and then working alongside a qualified and experienced pharmacist for a year – called registration. There are voluntary continuous training opportunities available to her, although these may soon be made compulsory for pharmacists.

Helen enjoys her work, especially being able to work with the public. She says that she would rather work in retail than in a hospital as she actually meets the people she administers drugs to. It was her ability to relate well to people that led to a friend suggesting that she should join the team of volunteer advisers at the local Citizen's Advice Bureau. She trained for 4–5 months and then joined the rota of volunteers. Now she does two sessions a week, from 9.30 – 1.00p.m., although after her 'shift' all cases must be written up for legal purposes and to enable other people to refer back if they pick up the case.

Volunteer advisers are a person's initial contact at the CAB. They do not counsel people, but they talk about their case and can then refer them to specialist helpers of all kinds. Helen says that there are lots of places to look up the information that is needed in giving advice, and that she has learnt a lot as she has gone along although the training did give some basic help in talking to and dealing with people.

Helen says she might have chosen a different job if she was able to start all over again, but she enjoys what she does. As a Jew, there are few jobs that she would not do. Some Jews work in non-kosher restaurants or teach home economics using non-kosher food, but she says that people doing these jobs need more self-control. Other Jews would feel unhappy doing these jobs. They would rather live in an area with other Jews and take a job in a wholly Jewish environment, for example, teaching in a Jewish school. She is very conscious of the fact that she is Jewish and especially that other people see her as a representative of Judaism – this means a feeling of responsibility. She is able to arrange life for her family so that they can celebrate their faith alongside other traditions in Britain. Her son, for example, goes to a school which has lessons on a Saturday morning, but special arrangements have been made to exempt him. She will not eat cooked food with non-Jewish friends because of Jewish kosher food laws, but will drink coffee and eat vegetarian food. She says that when you have grown up in a situation, then you get used to it.

INFORMATION SHEET 3c

WORKING IN THE COMMUNITY

Work in the Community – Daleep

Daleep is a Sikh. She works as a bilingual assistant at a local primary school, where 98 per cent of the pupils are Muslims. Most of the time they do not notice the difference, but every now and then they will comment if she wears a 'bindi' (a red 'spot' on her forehead, which is a mark of a married Sikh lady). The differences do not cause problems.

She started the job ten years ago as a classroom assistant, but gradually moved into the language work. She also works with children with special needs. Her job has gained in status over the years and is important as she is able to help pupils to understand concepts which might be difficult to those not brought up in the traditional British way of life. For instance, when the teacher talks about going on holiday to the seaside it makes little sense to Muslim children, but Daleep is able to liken it to going to India to see relatives. She can put things across in a different way for pupils.

At first there was no training and she simply helped in the classroom with packing away, etc., but now the teachers have realised a need for language support and training in dealing with children, and so Daleep and the other assistants are able to undertake training – often in their own time. She has recently gained a distinction pass in an RSA examination, which she is thrilled about. She says that she left school very early to get married and is pleased to be able to prove to herself now that she can learn again. She is currently half way through an NVQ (National Vocational Qualification).

She enjoys her work, and gains real satisfaction from seeing pupils develop, especially those who arrive unable to speak English and the following year are chattering away in it. 'I feel that I have changed something, and done something worthwhile', she says. It can be very hard work though, and there are times when she gets frustrated and feels that she could put something across better than a teacher because of her knowledge of the pupils' backgrounds.

Daleep is pleased to be able to take her faith into school, and to be able to explain aspects of it to pupils. She always says that if they do not understand why people do certain things, or wear things and so on, then they should ask. There are few jobs that a Sikh would not take on, although social work is not very popular. Until recently the wearing of the turban made it difficult for Sikh men to get into some professions. The Police Force have only just changed their laws to allow them to wear a black turban instead of the helmet, but Daleep says that it was a difficult fight to get this passed. One of her relatives went for a job interview at a town hall and was asked whether he thought that his turban would 'put people off'. He found it difficult to get a job.

All orthodox Sikhs will wear the five Ks, one of which is carrying a small dagger (a *kirpan*). This is hidden underneath clothing and does not usually pose a problem at work, although one of Daleep's friends is asked to take hers off on the airplane whenever she visits India. Orthodox Sikhs may also refuse to sell cigarettes and tobacco in their shops because such drugs are forbidden to them, and Daleep says that she would not work as a cook in a restaurant or school cafeteria which involved the cooking of *halal* or 'beef' meat as Sikhs do not eat these.

INFORMATION SHEET 3d

WORKING IN THE COMMUNITY

Work in the Community – Brenda

Brenda is a funeral director. She belongs to a Christian church and is an active member of a housegroup there. She did not go into the funeral business straight from school, but believes that she was guided there by God after being made redundant from a firm where she worked designing and making jewellery. She was looking for office work and asked her housegroup to pray for her – that she would find the right job. Someone remarked that, with her caring approach to people, she ought to be 'in the funeral business'. She saw an advert in the paper the next day for a receptionist at a local undertakers and applied. She was offered the job, and felt that it was the right place to be.

That was three years ago. After she had been with the firm for a while it was suggested that she should study for the diploma that undertakers may take. She travelled to London once a week for a year, with a colleague. She says that the two of them supported each other through the study which involved various projects such as making coffins, showing a group into a chapel of rest, and watching and writing up an embalming. There was also a lot of legal information to learn. At the end there was a national examination with both oral and written papers. She was very nervous, but passed and is now a branch administrator and a member of the British Institute of Funeral Directors.

Brenda's work involves all aspects of arranging a funeral – from meeting the family when they make the first contact to ordering flowers and making church or crematorium arrangements. She does not actually make the coffins and dress the bodies, as the firm has a separate team to do that. However, she has had to do so occasionally. For example, a Hindu family wanted a lady dressed in her sari and Brenda was called in to do that. She says that she has had to learn about the customs of faiths other than her own, so that she is able to be respectful and make sure that people feel comfortable in their time of grief.

Being a woman in the funeral business has not always been easy. Some people take her for the secretary when they call, but she believes that there is also a plus side to being a woman, it is easier and more acceptable for her to hold a hand or for people to cry in front of her. She has not often supervised the funeral on the day, but is beginning to do more of this. This means being in charge of the whole event on the day, from walking in front of the hearse to making sure that the service goes as planned, and that the committal is right. There are lots of little things to remember. She says that she gets very worried about this because she is keen that everything should be exactly as the family would like. 'People appreciate it when you make the effort.'

Brenda enjoys getting alongside people and being able to help them at a difficult time. Sometimes people will ring her after the funeral to chat. She says that the most difficult funerals to cope with personally are those where there is some personal link – either she knew the person or it was someone the same age as her children. She also finds it heartrending when one of an elderly couple, who have been married for many years dies. She admits that it is difficult to let go at home, but her church helps her to cope, and supports her. She sometimes gets her leg pulled at work about being a Christian, but she says that she could not do the job if she were not a Christian. She is able to pray for the families that she works with and tries to give them hope, through God.

As a Christian, there are some things that she would not do in a job, such as telling lies (she's 'out of the office', etc.) or working in a betting shop. She does not approve of working on Sundays, but would in this job, if it were necessary.

Brenda now sees her job as a vocation. It does not make her question her faith, as she is able to help others, but the death of a friend recently has had this effect. She knows that she will get through with the support of the church. When she sometimes feels that she is in the wrong job, often a letter will come through thanking her for what she has done for a family – and that makes it all worthwhile.

Copyright © 1996 by Sally Lynch. The Publishers grant permission for multiple copies of this page to be made for use solely within that institution.

INFORMATION SHEET 3e

WORKING IN THE COMMUNITY

Work in the Community – Ranjit

Ranjit is a Vayshanauvs. This group is seen as part of Hinduism, but he does not like the idea of a Hindu 'religion' as it is, he says, such a broad concept and too complex to pin down to the confines of a religion. The Vayshanauvs are outside the caste system, and Ranjit is very opposed to it, as he believes that it has caused many problems. He says that it is very difficult to practice Hinduism in the small city where he lives because there is no mandir (Hindu temple), and so people travel to larger cities where they can meet with bigger groups of Hindus. He believes that there is also a level of prejudice which prevents Hindus from fully practising their 'religion'.

His family did not approve of his chosen job at first, and now they are still only indifferent about it. Ranjit is a Police Officer. At the time that he left university, the Tottenham riots had just happened and it brought to the front of his mind the issue of justice and law. There was an ethnic minority recruitment drive in the Police Force, he had a degree and was welcomed to the Force. He joined under the graduate entry scheme, but most people join at 18 with GCSE and A levels, they must also sit a basic Police examination. After an initial interview there was then a final interview with the Deputy Chief Constable, and Ranjit was told that he had been accepted.

He followed a subdivision for a month to experience some Police life, and then went to training school for about three months, with a break back on the job to apply what he was learning. After this he became a probationary Constable for two years. Now he continues on-the-job training by going on courses as appropriate. There are many sections to the Police Force – the Patrol section, Community, Criminal Investigation Department, Traffic, and so on. It is also possible to gain promotion through the ranks of Police Officers, and Ranjit is keen to do this.

He is currently a Constable, but has a high level of responsibility and does some training of younger officers. He says that sometimes people will assume, if he is with a white officer, that the white officer is the superior. He says that he can cope with that, as there is no point in getting upset at prejudice. Following recent highly publicised problems in the Force, there are radical moves now being made to deal with racism, and the issue is covered in training too.

Ranjit says that he enjoys the job because he is able to look at society in a different light and to do something to help people. For example, dealing with domestic violence is a way of preventing people from doing wrong. Yet he says that it also makes him see the negative side of humanity and he feels that this has changed his character.

His parents were unhappy about his job as it is not viewed highly by many Hindus. The role of Inspector might be acceptable, but the mundane work of an officer does not fit well with the caste system that Ranjit would like to escape from. When he first joined the force he had some difficulties in dealing with sudden deaths, as it is considered unclean for Hindus to touch a dead body. After 12 years, he says that it has to be done, and he copes with it. He says that he finds worship difficult as it so often becomes a shopping list of requests. He wants to do something constructive with the life that he believes God has given him. His work as a Police Officer enables him to do that.

INFORMATION SHEET 3f

WORKING IN THE COMMUNITY

Work in the Community – Annette

Annette is an Orthodox Jew. She works as a medical counsellor, splitting her time between a hospice for the dying, and a large hospital. She was originally an orthoptist, but came to the conclusion that dealing with the physical aspect of an illness was only part of the healing process, and that the emotional aspects needed to be tackled too. What were simple illnesses to hospitals were life changing things to families and patients. A number of factors affected her, such as working with children with eye problems for whom wearing an eye patch caused huge emotional difficulties which prevented recovery, and the medical needs of her own family. She went back to university and took a postgraduate diploma in adult psycho-dynamic counselling.

Then she took up her present job, which is quite unusual. Annette works with patients and families to look after their emotional needs during their illness. She helps them to come to terms with the diagnosis, and the future. This sometimes involves bereavement work. She also does staff development and training and is beginning to work with medical students as well as being a liaison in the team of those involved with a patient. She offers emotional support to families through a support team and links with community services too. In all of this she works with teams of people.

Annette says that the best part of the job is that she is able to try to change things for the better and to help people in a time of NHS cutbacks. The worst part is that even if you did it 24 hours a day, it would never be enough. She has an outside supervisor whom she meets once a week, to give her the emotional support that she, in turn, needs.

While many people might say that they have come to this work as a vocation, Annette would not make that claim for herself. Rather she says that it is linked to her Jewish culture. Judaism is very community conscious and has certain *mitzvot* (things which one should try to do), which include giving, and enabling others to have dignity. She is able to do this through her work.

It is not easy being a practising Jew in a country which is not geared up to the regulations of Judaism. Annette says that when preparing for the Sabbath she has to be very organised as she cannot do things like shop on a Saturday. She has also been accused of going off early to do her shopping on a Friday in preparation for the Sabbath, but most of her colleagues now accept the religious reasons and, if anything, simply see her as slightly eccentric. She does feel uncomfortable about taking time off for Jewish holy days and so she always makes the time up or has to take it as part of her holiday. The advantage is that she is easily available on call at Christmas time! Yet she does feel that she misses out on much of the hospital social life which tends to happen on a Friday night.

Many of the issues that arise in Annette's work are spiritual issues relevant to all religions, but she is aware of her limitations and may feel it right to say to a patient that she is not the right person to talk to when they want to talk about Christian matters of life and death. She is called when a Jewish patient occasionally comes in, but she has to remind staff that there are many strands in Judaism, just as in Christianity, and an Orthodox Jew, for example, may not welcome a pastoral visit from a Reform Jew. She feels that her religion helps a lot on the issue of bereavement, as Judaism is very strong on mourning and support for the bereaved. Traditional British culture can expect people to get on with their lives too soon. The job could, however, cause problems for some very strict Jews because of the moral dilemmas often raised with respect to when a life should be allowed to end – Judaism teaches that life should always be prolonged.

Annette says that she enjoys her work, and would not take up a job which would not enable her to fulfil the responsibilities of her Jewish way of life. She would not work in a non-kosher restaurant or do some types of shift work, although doctors and nurses are allowed to break that religious requirement in order to save life. She is able to live out fully the requirements of Judaism to minister to others through her unique work.

WORKING IN THE COMMUNITY

Work in the Community – Dhiranandi

Dhiranandi works in a shop. Yet she would not call herself a shop assistant in the usual use of the term. She works in one of the ten shops in the Evolution chain, which is run by Windhorse Trading Ltd. She is also a member of the Western Buddhist Order and so has the title Dharmacharini which means follower of the Dharma or teaching of the Buddha. This means she has committed herself to the ideal of Enlightenment which every human being can attain – a state of perfect wisdom, compassion and energy. To do this means she lives out the precepts or principles of loving kindness, generosity and awareness in every aspect of her life, including, of course, her work.

For some years she followed the Buddha's teachings in Lancashire. After working in a hospital and then with deaf people, she set up a window cleaning business which meant she could work with other Buddhists in conditions which would enable her to live out those Buddhist principles. She says that it is not just a case of what work you do, but how you do it is also important to Buddhists. Later she wanted to deepen her friendships with other women who were ordained into the Western Buddhist Order and was invited to move south to work in a newly set up branch of Evolution.

The shop is a team-based 'Right Livelihood'. There is no manager and the workers could just as easily be painting the walls as serving customers or doing the buying. In each of the shops people work in teams with people of the same sex because they have found that this is the best way to deepen friendships with each other and develop their Buddhist practice together. There is no real difference between religion and work.

Windhorse Trading started as a market stall in Camden town in 1984. It grew into a wholesale business in order to raise money for the building of the London Buddhist Centre and to enable Buddhists to work together. In 1991 they decided to open some shops of their own too. The work is not just normal shop work, it is about using one's creativity, learning to co-ooperate with each other and developing ideas which will help the shop to run more efficiently and to help the customers to find and buy what they want, i.e. doing better displays etc. Many people comment on the difference when they enter the shops, although they may not know why it is.

Dhiranandi lives in a women's spiritual community with five other Windhorse Trading workers. They do not earn a normal wage, but take only what they need to live on, plus a little pocket money. Working is not just for a living, but an opportunity to develop oneself. Generosity is also important to Buddhists. Profits are given away to Buddhist charities. Last year Dhiranandi's branch was able to give away £35,000 and the business as a whole £86,000.

All those who work in the shop work a five-day week with six weeks a year as retreat time. Dhiranandi has just returned from two weeks solitary retreat in Spain – giving her time to meditate, study and experience herself more fully. She believes that this space is important for all people. 'Most people are so busy doing, that they have little time to just be.'

She says that the best part of her life and work is that it creates a different way of relating to the world and provides good conditions for other peoples' working lives too: conditions in which people can really give and develop the best in themselves. There are no real drawbacks, she says, as there will always be problems in life and the challenge is to overcome them. For those Buddhists not as lucky as she is to have the opportunity of working together in such a team, she says that they would have to weigh up the jobs open to them and not take on work that would be harmful to others and that fit with the teachings of the Buddha. They would have to think very carefully before doing work where they would be expected to experiment on animals, if they were a chemist for example, or to work in some jobs where too much bureaucracy compromised what would otherwise be very helpful work.

In the same way the Evolution chain are careful who they buy from, they do not buy or sell shell, leather or silk products. Most people who trade with them are impressed by their honesty and good communication. Dhiranandi finds her work creative, and a way of giving back to the world. It is far more than a career where one simply gets out of it what one can. It is about developing as a person by working with, and for, the good of others.

INFORMATION SHEET 3h

WORKING IN THE COMMUNITY

Work in the Community – Razahusein

Razahusein is a chartered accountant running his own firm with six employees. He is a Muslim and is very involved in his local mosque. The mosque is a large, purpose built, building which serves the local community of about 1000 Muslims, and Razahusein also shows round groups of local school children and helps them to understand more about his religion.

He came to England when he was 15 and did A levels in this country before going on to higher education. He then went through the usual training for an accountant which means gaining a training contract and working with a firm for 3–4 years, studying and doing exams at this time. An accountant then needs to find a job. This is not usually as difficult as getting the training contract to start with, and there are also plenty of vacancies abroad for English trained accountants. Razahusein worked for a firm and was a manager for some years before setting up his own business in 1981. His work involves preparing and auditing accounts for businesses and assisting them with their tax affairs. He is basically a tax and financial adviser. He says that he finds a real job satisfaction from being able to help clients to set up and run businesses.

Razahusein finds no conflict between his job and his faith. He says that Islam is a very practical religion and that both business and personal ethics affect his professional life for good. The Qur'an says a lot about the way that business people should treat clients and so he is very careful to try to treat his clients fairly, for example, in the way that they are charged.

Teachings on personal issues are also important. A Muslim must observe five times of prayer each day which reminds him that Allah is involved in the whole of his life. The midday prayers occur during the working day, but timings are flexible enough to fit in with lunchtimes, although on a Friday there are special *Jumma* prayers at the mosque and Razahusein will make a point of going to these. His employees know that they should not make appointments for him at this time. The Qur'an also teaches that Muslims must not drink alcohol and so he will not go out for a drink with clients, but finds that once they know the reason for this, they respect his practice. This is also true of the time during Ramadan when he will be fasting during the daytime.

Only two of his employees are also Muslim. Others are Hindu and Christian, and sometimes they talk about their different religions as each has different days off for their festivals. He finds this valuable and believes that it is often ignorance which leads to prejudice. This is why he is so keen to take time off from his business to work with groups of children at the mosque. He believes that once the initial hurdles are overcome, then people of different religions work well together. They need to understand and respect each other's religious practices.

As a Muslim there are a few jobs which he would not do. These are jobs which might be harmful to humanity at large. So he would not work in any trade which sold or promoted alcohol, or drugs or gambling. However, most jobs are open to him and he says that Islam is flexible enough to allow him to practice his faith alongside his work.

WORKSHEET 3

WORKING IN THE COMMUNITY

Work in the Community

1. a) Read or listen to at least two of the Information Sheets which give accounts of different religious people at work.

   b) Find a partner and each of you take the role of one of the people in the Information Sheets. As that person, explain to your partner what your job involves and how your religion affects your work.

2. Choose one of the jobs or religions that interests you. Find out more about it by using your careers library or textbooks. Make notes and tell someone else what you have found out.

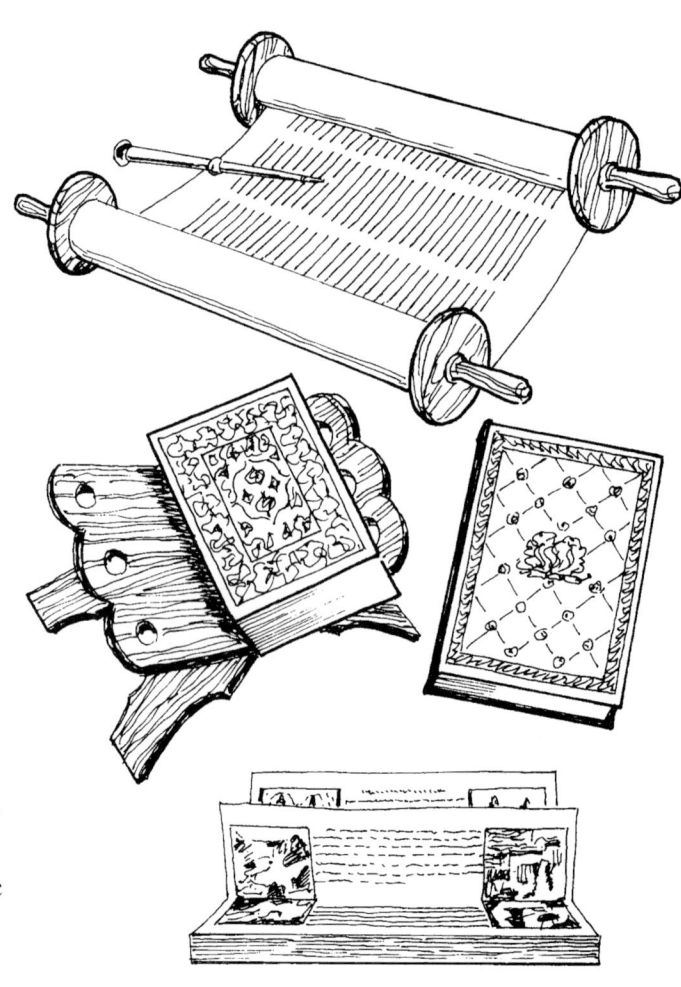

3. In a group, look at all of the sheets and compare them.
   a) Are there some aspects of all religions which affect the way that followers do their jobs?
   b) Are there some jobs that it would be wrong for all religious people to do?
   c) Discuss as a class the answers that the groups come up with. Do you think that being 'religious' makes a person a better worker?

4. Work with a partner. If you were able to interview any of the people you have studied, what extra questions would you like to ask them? Try to find out the answers by asking local people of that religion, or people who do that job.

5. Think about the sort of job that you might like to do in the future. Are there any aspects of your own, or other people's religious belief and practice, that might make it difficult to do?

6. Religious people look in their holy books for advice about their jobs. Choose a religion and find out what its holy book says about work.

INFORMATION SHEET 4

WORKING IN THE COMMUNITY

Vocation and Talent

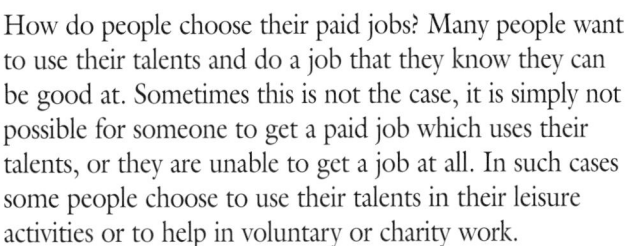

How do people choose their paid jobs? Many people want to use their talents and do a job that they know they can be good at. Sometimes this is not the case, it is simply not possible for someone to get a paid job which uses their talents, or they are unable to get a job at all. In such cases some people choose to use their talents in their leisure activities or to help in voluntary or charity work.

Whatever their gifts are, and wherever they use them, many religious people believe that it is important to make the most of gifts that they believe have been given by God. This is called stewardship. A steward is someone who looks after something, or does something, for someone else. At a wedding, a steward will show people to their places and look after them on behalf of the bride and groom. So in a religious sense, there is a belief that God has given people many things (time, talents, money, homes etc.) and that they should use them to the best of their ability in the service of God. This will usually mean seeking advice in their Holy Book or from their religious leaders about the best way to use the gifts that they have.

In medieval times in Britain a number of groups grew up in the cities called 'guilds'. These were associations of craftsmen who shared the same talents. The guilds enabled them to develop and share their talents. This is a little similar to today's Trade Unions, although these also have an important role in the fair treatment of workers in all areas of employment.

Some religious people take the idea of talents one step further and believe that they are called to a particular job by God. This is called 'vocation'. It is the idea that God has given someone a particular gift which they feel that they must use to serve him. For some people this is through 'ordinary' jobs. For example, a woman might feel that she has a vocation to be a doctor so that she can use the medical skills that she has developed in order to help others. For other people this might mean giving up a 'normal' family life and becoming a monk or a nun, giving full time service to God in prayer or practical work. Some Christians would say that in the 1990s Terry Waite was a man with a vocation from God. He used his gift of mediation to help free hostages, in God's name, and did not give up even when his own life was in danger.

WORKSHEET 4

WORKING IN THE COMMUNITY

Vocation and Talent

1. Design large posters for the wall, which explain clearly what 'talents' and 'vocation' are. Use pictures to help.

2. a) What are your talents? List the things that you are good at. (If you find this difficult work with a friend and help each other.)

   b) How could you build on these talents, develop them, or use them in the future?

3. a) Read the parable of the talents in the Bible, Matthew 25:14-30.

   b) Role play the story with a group OR write your own version OR talk about the story in a group.

4. Discuss in groups how you think that schools today could help young people to make the most of their talents.

5. Discuss in groups whether you agree that talents can be given by God.

6. Do you know anyone who has a vocation? Invite someone into school to answer questions and explain what vocation means to them. It could be a local priest, or nurse, or even one of your teachers.

7. a) Find out more about a famous person who has shown that they have a vocation. E.g. Mother Teresa; Julia Neuberger; Jackie Pullinger.

   b) Present your findings in an interesting way; e.g. cartoon strip, mock interview.

WORKSHEET 5

WORKING IN THE COMMUNITY

People at Work

In small groups, each take a role from the list of opinions below and role play it with the others. Argue against each other – but you must stay in role. Try to think about how people with such arguments would speak out.

Then discuss them with each other.
- Why are they potentially very damaging in the world of work?
- How do they relate to the idea of equal opportunities?
- How do they fit in with religious ideas and values? Do the teachings on Information Sheet 5 have anything to say to these situations?

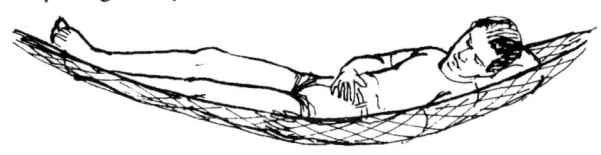

'It's alright to take a few days off now and then, I need to recharge my batteries, and everyone does it.'

'I would never have a woman working in the workshop with me. They can't cope with the physical side, and anyway, they would be distracting – know what I mean!'

'Men can't be hairdressers – it makes them poofs. You can't gossip to a man in the hairdressers.'

'She won't make it to managing director. You have to have really good A levels. She hasn't, and her parents live in the East End of London. I don't think women have the same authority as men either.'

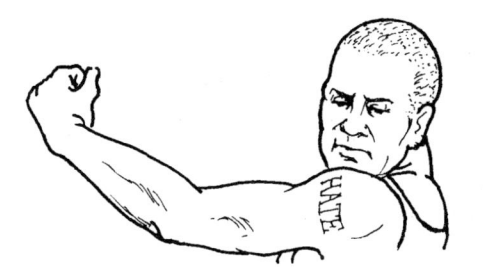

'I didn't get into the Police Force because of my tattoo. I don't think it's fair – it's discrimination – it is part of my personality to have HATE tatooed on my arm.'

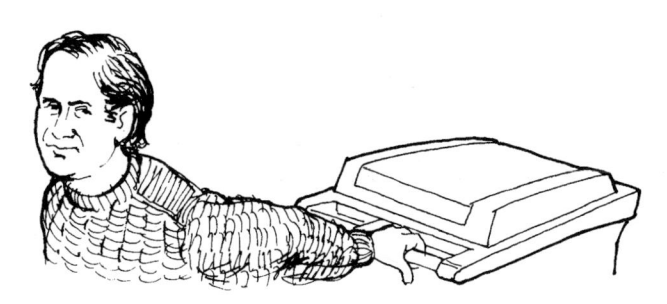

'You don't want to go out with her, her Dad is a refuse collector. You might catch something.'

'I wish I could climb higher in my job, there seem to be no openings for me. What else must I do?'

Copyright © 1996 by Sally Lynch. The Publishers grant permission for multiple copies of this page to be made for use solely within that institution.

INFORMATION SHEET 5

WORKING IN THE COMMUNITY
People at Work

It is almost too obvious to say it, but work is about people. We have computers, animals and machines that work 'for' us, but they ultimately have to be worked 'by' us. That is, we have to set them up in the right way so that they do what we want them to.

We have seen that religions are also about people, and that religions care about the way that people are treated at work. They want people to have work to do so that they can feel valued and take a full part in their community. Religions are based on certain values and beliefs. As we saw in the case studies, these beliefs will affect attitudes in all areas of life, work is one of them.

BUDDHISM

In following the eightfold path, Buddhists try to live by a 'Right Livelihood'. In practice this means that they will avoid any work which will cause harm to any other living being. Work is necessary in order to support self and family, but it must be honest. To help Buddhists in countries such as Britain, the Friends of the Western Buddhist Order have set up businesses on 'Right Livelihood' lines.

CHRISTIANITY

There are no such strict guidelines about work here, although the Bible makes it clear that work is important and that it is good. The punishments on Adam and Eve for disobeying God at creation (see Genesis 3:14-24) make it clear that work will also be hard at times. Yet Christians should work to support both themselves and the community (see 2 Thessalonions 3:7-12). Some of their earnings should also go to those who cannot work.

HINDUISM

The work that a Hindu does is determined by his or her caste, with physical and manual work being considered as less dignified than office work. Most women stay at home, although this is changing today, especially in the West. Hindus are also encouraged to work hard. 'Work in such a way that you forget the stresses and strains of success or failure. This way of living is the best kind of devotion. Those who live any other way will be unhappy.' (Bhagavad Gita 2:48).

ISLAM

Muslims must also work hard to support their families: 'No one eats better food than that which they have earned by their own labours' (Hadith). All work is considered to be honourable and all jobs are equal, although any work which would result in loss or hurt to another person is banned (e.g: selling alcohol, prostitution etc.). Muslims must also pay fair wages to employees and not charge interest on loans.

JUDAISM

Work is also important for Jews in order to bring self-respect and to use one's creative gifts. Everyone should work (see Proverbs 18:9 and Proverbs 6:6-11) but not on the Sabbath as that is when God rested at creation, and people too need a rest. Work should be honest and not harmful to others.

SIKHISM

To Sikhs no work is to be considered as beneath them. All work is to be for the good of humanity. It is a religious duty therefore, and a way of serving God. Sikhs should not withdraw from the world to pray all the time, but they should work in it for its improvement.

In many religions this concern for hard, self-supporting work also applies to their religious leaders and priests. In Judaism, Islam and Sikhism the religious leaders are expected to work alongside their religious studies and not to be reliant on others for their upkeep. There is also a concern in all religions for hard work, alongside earned rest, which gives a person worth and value.

INFORMATION SHEET 6

WORKING IN THE COMMUNITY

Money

> Some of us seem incredibly inconsistent when it comes to giving cash to God's work. On the one hand we claim to have given our lives to the Lord, but we don't let him have our wallets.
> — Cliff Richard

> Money doesn't grow on trees.
> — Anon

> Where there's muck, there's money.
> — Anon

> Money is like muck, not good except it be spread.
> — Francis Bacon

> How pleasant it is to have money.
> — A.H. Clough

> The love of money is the root of all evil.
> — St Paul (1 Timothy 6:10)

> Money makes the world go round
> — Anon

> It is pretty to see what money will do.
> — Samuel Pepys

> Up and down the City Road,
> In and out the Eagle,
> That's the way the money goes –
> Pop goes the weasel!
> — W.R. Mandale

Paid employment gives us money. We earn wages. We get a salary, a pay packet, a cheque. We may get state financial benefits. We may inherit a fortune. We may get pocket money. We have money.

Yet money in itself does us no good. Money is amoral. It cannot be good or bad on its own. It is what we DO with our money, and our attitude towards it that makes money good or bad. Some people have lots of money, others have very little, a few have none. Some have plenty to live on and lots left over, others have just enough, others can't manage on what they have.

Money can be used to buy the things we need to live – food, clothes and shelter. It can purchase things that make life comfortable – cars, holidays and CDs. It can be used for extra luxuries or to give to those who don't have enough.

The sayings above show some of the different attitudes that people have towards money. You might like to think about them. You can probably also think of pop songs written about money. You might listen to some.

Copyright © 1996 by Sally Lynch. The Publishers grant permission for multiple copies of this page to be made for use solely within that institution.

WORKSHEET 6

WORKING IN THE COMMUNITY
Money

1. a) In pairs make a list of all of the ways that money can be used well.
   b) Now make a list of all of the ways that money can be abused.
   c) Join together with another pair and make two long lists of the ways that money can be used well or abused.
   d) Find as many newspaper cuttings as you can to illustrate each list. Use them to make posters showing the use and abuse of money.

2. a) Look at the sayings about money on Information Sheet 6. Try to explain in your own words what each means.
   b) Discuss your explanations with a partner. Do you agree with each saying? Explain your views to your partner.
   c) Can you think of any more sayings about money that you have heard, or that you can make up between you?

3. a) What would you do if you won £10,000?
   b) Ask different people (not only in school) the same question.
   c) What sort of answers did you get?
   d) Did young or older people give different answers?
   e) Why do you think people answered as they did?
   f) Discuss your answers with a partner.

4. a) Write out your weekly or monthly budget. How much do you get and what do you spend it on?
   b) Now imagine that you are working and earning a wage. You have a family to support. List all that you will need to budget for.
   c) Is there any money left in each case? What will, or do, you do with it?

5) Discuss with a partner what you would do if you had no money.

6) Jesus encouraged people to share their money with others. For some this was possible, for others it was very difficult.
   a) Read the story of the rich young man in Luke 19:18-23.
   b) Now re-tell the story in your own words, but add an ending – what DID the young man do?
   c) You might like to read Jesus' words to the crowd as the young man left, in Luke 19:24-30. [In v. 25 he speaks about a camel going through the eye of a needle. This may refer to a tiny gate in the city wall nicknamed the eye of the needle and which it was impossible to get a camel through. A touch of humour for his listeners – to get across a serious point.]

Copyright © 1996 by Sally Lynch. The Publishers grant permission for multiple copies of this page to be made for use solely within that institution.

INFORMATION SHEET 7

WORKING IN THE COMMUNITY
Religions and Wealth

As we have seen, we earn money by working (and other means). 'Wealth' is what we might buy with our money – it is the goods that we accumulate. How do religious people feel about wealth? A saying from 1 Timothy is often misquoted – people say that money is the root of all evil when what St Paul actually says is that the LOVE of money causes evil. This is important for religious people. Religions do not say that money is bad because by itself money can do no good or harm; but religious people are very concerned about how that money is used, and about 'fair shares' for all people.

'To me, desire for money and wealth stems from basic human greed. I feel that my life is rich when I live a good life, following the principles of Buddhism. Material wealth can bring me only unhappiness and a craving for more. I enjoy my possessions, but I want to share what I have and be generous to ensure a good future life. I like especially to give food to the Buddhist monks who have chosen to give up nearly all possessions.'

'I am lucky enough to have a well paid job, but I follow Jesus' teachings to share what I have with those less fortunate. I believe that I should tithe my income, following the example of the first Christians. I ask God to show me how to use my wealth – Jesus said "You cannot serve God and money" (Matthew 6:24).'

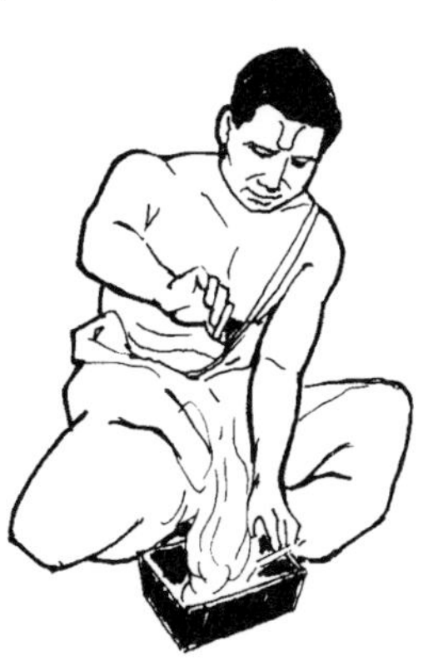

'There are four aims in my life. The second is *artha* (gaining wealth by lawful means). It is bound up with the others too – *kama* (enjoying the good things of life) and with *dharma* (living in the right way) and *moksha* (freedom from this life). So, you see, I must earn and spend money honestly and without harming others. I must also carry out five daily obligations, one of which is to give shelter to guests. I do this by giving to a charity which will benefit the poor.'

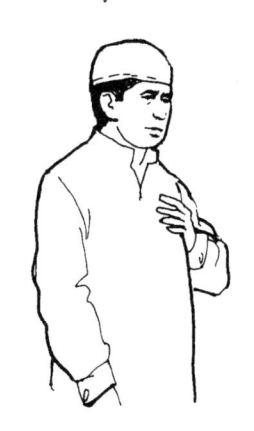

'My religion teaches that wealth which is honestly gained is to be honoured. But I also have a religious duty to share it with the poor. This *zakat* is a tax of 2.5 per cent of my income. I choose to give to charity on top of this. Muhammad said "He who eats and drinks while his brother goes hungry, is not one of us".'

'I see nothing wrong with earning money and having wealth, as long as it is gained fairly. I must give 10 per cent of my income to charity though, and there are a number of ways of doing this. The best way is to give so that I do not know who it is going to and he does not know that it is from me. Even though I do not earn much, I am still required to give to charity. If I could take a poor person into business and help them to have a better life that would be ideal.'

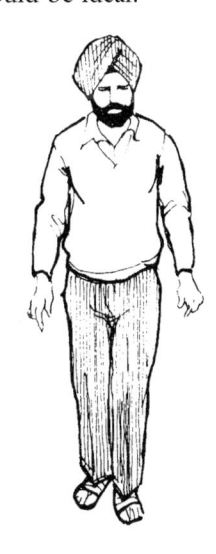

'Guru Nanak set many examples to show what our attitude should be towards wealth. Although it is good to provide the means to live, it cannot be taken into the next world. It must also be earned honestly. I must also give 10 per cent of my income to charity and this particularly goes to help run the *langar* (free kitchen) at my gurdwara. This is open to anyone.'

WORKSHEET 7

WORKING IN THE COMMUNITY
Religions and Wealth

1. Imagine that you are a religious believer with a family. You earn £900 a month. Write an account of how you would allocate your income each month to fit in with the teachings of your religion about money and wealth.

2. a) Find out more about the teachings of two or more religions about wealth. Make a chart to show your findings.
   b) Do these religions agree with each other?
   c) Do you agree with them?
   d) Why do you think they teach what they do?

3. a) Look up these Bible teachings about wealth and match up the references to the captions. One has been done for you.

4. a) Most religions teach about stewardship – the idea that a believer's wealth is given by God and that they are simply looking after it for him. Therefore they should use it for the benefit of others too – as God would want them to. Do you agree with this idea?
   b) Prepare notes and debate the motion:
   This house believes that my money is my own, to do with as I like.

   b) Draw a cartoon collage to show what the Bible or another religion's holy book has to say about wealth (or you could cut suitable pictures from magazines to form a collage).

Leviticus 27:30	You can't take it with you
Amos 8:4-6	Give a tithe to charity
Matthew 6:1-4	The early church shared possessions
Matthew 6:19-21	Don't just pray for people in need
Mark 12:41-44	It's giving that counts – however little you have to give
Luke 12:13-21	Don't make a show of giving
James 2:14-17	Don't hoard!
Acts 4:32-37	Even in Old Testament times the poor were being cheated

INFORMATION SHEET 8

WORKING IN THE COMMUNITY

Leisure

You may have heard the saying 'all work and no play makes Jack a dull boy'. It is probably very true. Most of us can think of people we know who do nothing but swot for tests or do homework or bring their work home. They can be very boring to be with. They might find it difficult to get on with other people. (They might also be quite unfit.) Human beings need to work to earn money to live on and to gain self-respect, but they also need to have time for leisure and rest.

WHY DO WE NEED LEISURE TIME?

- *to rest our minds which are taxed at work*
- *to take physical exercise and improve our bodies (it can also be relaxing!)*
- *to meet with other people and make new friends, being sociable*
- *to meet new challenges and ambitions*
- *to be with our families and strengthen relationships*
- *to make time for others or to help others*
- *to worship God without being rushed*
- *to rest our bodies and build up our strength through sleep*
- *to spend time in reflection about ourselves and the direction of our lives*
- *to work out the frustrations of our job*
- *to be creative and use our talents*

People use their leisure time differently and each of the reasons for leisure above might be fulfilled in a number of activities. Some people seem to work harder in their leisure time than at work – on hobbies such as running or home DIY. Other people choose to spend some of their time helping others in a voluntary capacity. There are a lot of important jobs in society which are only done in this way. Others spend time raising money for charities or caring for our environment. If the community is going to function fully then all people in it need to work for it, but also to have time for leisure together so that other tasks can be undertaken and they can themselves be recreated and refreshed to keep going.

Copyright © 1996 by Sally Lynch. The Publishers grant permission for multiple copies of this page to be made for use solely within that institution.

WORKSHEET 8

WORKING IN THE COMMUNITY

Leisure

1. a) Think about how you spend your leisure time. Make a list of all that you do in a week.
   b) Copy out the circle of reasons for leisure from Information Sheet 8 and see if you can write something that you do in each segment. If there are blanks, is there anything that you could start doing to fill them?
   c) Could you do any more with your leisure time (or should you do less!)?

2. Plan a week's leisure activities suitable for a religious believer which includes all or most of the types of leisure. (see Information Sheet 9 for help.) Say why you have planned your week as you have.

3. Find out which jobs in society are voluntary and unpaid. Make a list. (You may be able to get some people to come and talk to you about what they do e.g. First Aid, conservation, meals on wheels.)

4. For one week every May people give up their spare time to put envelopes like the one below through every door in Britain, and then to go back and collect them. The envelopes are to put money in for Christian Aid – a charity which helps people in need in the Developing World.

For some years Margaret was a collector during Christian Aid week. Why did she give up her time to do this?

'Well it's only for one week, although I do find it difficult to fit it around my family commitments. But I enjoy meeting new people and being able to do just a little to help others, despite the dogs that bark when I walk up some paths! It is rewarding to know that I can give some time to do something practical as I can't go out to those countries and help there myself. I am grateful for all the material things that I have and I want to use some of my spare time as a way of thanking God and showing my gratitude'.

   a) Do you agree with Margaret's attitude?
   b) Find out more about the work of Christian Aid, or another charity which relies on voluntary work. Present your findings in an interesting way, such as a chart or a tape recording or a cartoon strip.

5. Design a poster which encourages people to use some of their leisure time for the benefit of others too.

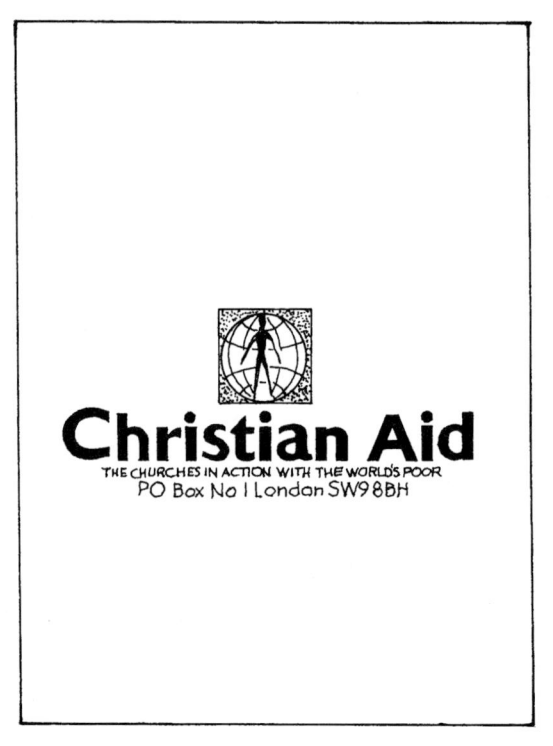

INFORMATION SHEET 9

WORKING IN THE COMMUNITY

Religions and Leisure

Christianity and Judaism both believe that God created human beings and, if this is so, then he knows how best we function. He knows that we need a time of rest and leisure if we are going to be able to live life to the fullest. It is for this reason that he instituted the Sabbath – a day off from work for rest and worship. People need a balance of activities which include all of the reasons for leisure if they are going to achieve what Jesus promised. 'I have come that you may have life – life in all its fullness.' (John 10:10b)

BUDDHISM

For Buddhists harmful use of leisure time and wasteful time is considered to be wrong, but rest and recreation are important for spiritual development. There is no set day on which to worship but most Buddhists try to set aside some time during each day for meditation. All life is dedicated to the principles of Buddhism and practising right livelihood.

CHRISTIANITY

There are no actual guidelines about how Christians should use their leisure time, but most would agree that it should be positive and not harmful to others or the environment. Some would disagree with forms of gambling and blood sports. Sunday has become the day on which Christians worship together. This recalls Jesus' resurrection and the first day of creation – both events emphasising the power of God in creation and inspiring worship of the creator.

HINDUISM

As earning money (*artha*) is one of the aims of Hindu life, so also is *kama*, or leisure. Hindus believe that people should keep a balance between work and enjoyment. Hindu festivals are often joyful and exciting times of celebration with families and friends sharing food and dancing together. This draws together leisure and the religious life. Much Hindu worship happens in the home, although communities do gather together in the *mandir* to worship. In Britain the day for this is usually Sunday when most people are free and able to join in.

ISLAM

Leisure time is important to Muslims too, so as to ensure a balance in life. Yet leisure activities should be appropriate and not harmful. There are four permitted sports in Islam: footracing, wrestling, archery and horseriding (or watching races). This does place some limits on women in a very strict or traditional community as they cannot take part in leisure activities which would bring them into contact with men. Islam has no special holy day, Muslims pray five times a day every day; but the prayers at midday on Friday are considered to be special and the *imam* (priest) will often give a sermon after them. For this reason many Muslim men try to get to the Jumma prayers on Friday. In Britain they will do this as far as possible.

JUDAISM

The fourth commandment is probably one of the most well known, Jews are told by God that they must 'Keep the Sabbath holy' (Exodus 20:8) . This means, according to Jewish belief and practice, a day off every week, to remember the seventh day when God rested from the creation of the world. This day is seen as a God-given gift when Jews are able to rest and, importantly, to worship too. Forms of leisure that are immodest, obscene or harmful are banned. Some Jews are very strict in their interpretation of what is work and will not cook or watch television on the Sabbath. Others are more liberal in their outlook. The day is sometimes called the 'Sabbath Bride' because it is so special. Families get together at the start of Sabbath, sunset on Friday night, and a traditional meal is held. Strangers and those alone are invited to join in. On the Saturday morning the men, or the whole family, will attend the synagogue service. In Britain Jews may organise their work so that it is possible to celebrate this weekly family festival.

SIKHISM

Sikhs also see leisure as important in enjoying a whole life and will encourage sporting activity and music making. Guru Nanak spoke out against watching plays and dancing, so some Sikhs will avoid this. There are certain restrictions on things that Sikhs may do in their leisure time – they may not gamble, drink alcohol or smoke. There is no set holy day and so congregational worship in the gurdwara can happen on any day, in Britain this is usually Sunday.

WORKSHEET 9a

WORKING IN THE COMMUNITY

Religions and Leisure

1. Look at the information about religious teachings about leisure.
   a) Are there any similarities in the teachings of the different religions?
   b) If so, what are they?
   c) Why do you think this is?

2. Imagine that you are a community worker in a multi-faith community. Write a leaflet, or make a tape, that you could distribute to employers outlining the teachings of different religions about leisure and worship requirements. Explain in it how any employer could make life at work most comfortable for employees of all religions. Explain what arrangement he/she might make to help people of all religions to follow their religion. (See also Information Sheet 3).

3. In pairs design a poster which illustrates leisure activities that might be both encouraged and discouraged by religious people. Say whether you agree with these things and why?

4. a) Look at these newspaper headlines:

In 1993 the British Government attempted to change the Sunday Trading laws to allow certain shops to open on Sundays. The laws were old and had lots of odd points in them. They needed changing. Yet many religious people were concerned about what they might be changed to and the effect that it would have on their religions and on society in general. There were four options before Parliament when they voted:
- total deregulation (any shop could open at any time);
- partial deregulation (shops over a certain size could open for up to 6 hours);
- partial deregulation with conditions (certain types of shop, selling certain goods could open);
- Christmas opening – any shop could open for the four Sundays before Christmas.

The second option was passed and became law in 1994.

b) Discuss what effect this might have on society, and all religious groups, especially Christians.

c) Use the debate arguments (from Information Sheet 9) to prepare and debate the motion:
This house believes that unlimited Sunday trading is acceptable in modern Britain.

Why must the weekend come to a dead stop?

SUNDAY – FUN DAY?

END THE TALKING AND LET THE SHOPS OPEN

GOING SHOPPING: But is it never on a Sunday?

INFORMATION SHEET 9

WORKING IN THE COMMUNITY
Religions and Leisure

SUNDAY TRADING DEBATE ARGUMENTS

For	Against
This is no longer a Christian country – why do we need to stick to Christian principles?	Families will be divided because one member is working.
Only about 5 per cent of the population go to church, and just a few more to other places of worship.	This is still a Christian country – look at the established church (Church of England).
People need jobs – this will ease unemployment.	People who want to go to church or services of worship will have difficult and unfair choices to make.
Shops can make more money.	Religious services will be disrupted by noise etc.
There is a demand for Sunday trading.	Sunday will become just like any other day, with no break in the weekly routine.
If people work in the rest of the week they want to be able to go out shopping with their family on Sundays.	Shops will have higher overheads and so charge higher prices.
Times have changed, so have the leisure needs of people. Shopping can be relaxing.	It will not solve unemployment, but create more part-time workers with lower wages.
What about emergency needs? The corner shop is too expensive.	Small shopkeepers will lose out.

INFORMATION SHEET 10

WORKING IN THE COMMUNITY
A Balanced Life

This unit has looked at the whole concept of work. We have seen different types of work and the difference between paid employment and other work. We have seen examples of jobs that people do, and you may have been out of school on work experience. We have seen that some people feel that they are called to do a particular job – they have a vocation, while others may spend a fair bit of their leisure time working in a voluntary way. Money is earned by work, and our attitudes toward money are important. We also need leisure time to relax and enable us to go back to our work refreshed and able to work more productively.

Religions have a lot to say about each of these issues. Religions believe that people are special, and to be valued as individuals. They believe that people have a right to work, to wealth and to leisure so that they can lead a full life. Only when all of these things are in a right balance can human beings really lead a whole and fulfilled life.

That does not mean that because someone is unemployed, they are not leading a full life, they may be; but ideally we need all of these aspects in our life if we are going to get the very best out of life. In Britain the government recognised this when it passed the 1988 Education Reform Act. This said that schools should prepare students for an adult life in terms of their spiritual, moral, cultural, mental and physical development.

Religions seem to be working towards just that, and provide lots of guidance too for their followers to help them work this out in practice. Jesus said that he had come so that people could live life to the fullest. We do that in the context of the community – all working, resting and playing together. We need each other to develop in each of these aspects – life would be pretty boring otherwise.

64 Copyright © 1996 by Sally Lynch. The Publishers grant permission for multiple copies of this page to be made for use solely within that institution.

WORKSHEET 10

WORKING IN THE COMMUNITY

A Balanced Life

1. Discuss the Information Sheet with a partner.
   a) Do you agree that we need many aspects of our life in balance in order to have a full life?
   b) What might happen if work and leisure were out of balance? (for example, if someone were unemployed or was working for 10 hours a day with few holidays).

2. a) Think about the aspects of adult life which the Education Act says schools should be preparing you for. Try to find out and explain to a partner what each of these means in reality:
   spiritual   moral   cultural
   mental   physical
   b) As a class discuss how this relates to your answers to task 1.

3. Think back over this unit of work, and look at your work.
   a) What did you learn from it about yourself and about others?
   b) What do you want to get out of your life?
   c) How do you plan to achieve it?
   d) Record your answers to these questions in some way. Share them with a partner if you wish to.

4. Design a leaflet, or make a tape or a video, which might be given to young people when they leave school. It will help them to look at the adult community and at how they might get the most out of life.
   Include advice and suggestions about:
   - working with others, types of work;
   - leisure and the need for it;
   - making time for others;
   - money and the use of it;
   - time for reflection and considering a purpose to life.

   Try to include some religious teachings or advice. Present it in a way that will appeal to young people. (You might include real or made up interviews, cartoons, story strips, a wordsearch, problem page – with answers . . .)

Section C

PEOPLE AROUND US IN THE COMMUNITY

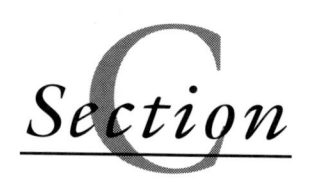

NOTES FOR THE TEACHER

AIMS AND OBJECTIVES

Aims:

- to look at the way in which people relate to others, and specific areas of breakdown;
- to study the teachings and advice of religions on these issues.

Objectives

Knowledge of:

- some problems that people face because of other people, e.g. prejudice;
- the work of agencies which help;
- examples of modern religious people who care for others;
- the teachings of religions about working together.

Understanding of:

- reasons for inhumanity to people;
- why people stand up for certain rights;
- religious teachings about right and freedom;
- what is important to me.

Ability to:

- explore further personal concerns;
- empathise with others;
- formulate and express an opinion clearly;
- reflect on important issues;
- research issues and report back clearly;
- relate issues discussed to local examples.

Experience of:

- role plays.

CONTENTS

Wordlist

1. People Around Us
   Information Sheet 1: introduction – pictures of local, national, international communities
   Worksheet 1: classify pictures, discussion

2. Religious Prejudice
   Information Sheet 2a: Judaism
   Information Sheet 2b: Samaritans
   Information Sheet 2c: Northern Ireland
   Information Sheet 2d: The Ba'hai
   Information Sheet 2e: Religious Teachings
   Worksheet 2: research further

3. Sexual Prejudice
   Information Sheet 3: case studies
   Worksheet 3: discussion tasks and poster

4. Racial Prejudice
   Information Sheet 4: British examples
   Worksheet 4: further (local) research and Bible

5. Persecution and Faith in the Past
   Information Sheet 5a: Masada
   Worksheet 5: reflective tasks
   Information Sheet 5b: Eleazar's Speech

6. Persecution Today
   Information Sheet 6: Amnesty International
   Worksheet 6: local research, tasks

7. Oppression Today
   Information Sheet 7: Bosnia
   Worksheet 7: national/local research

8. Human Rights
   Worksheet 8: task looking at rights in the local community
   Information Sheet 8: UN charter of Human Rights

9. Handicap
   Worksheet 9a: brainstorm and attitudes
   Information Sheet 9a: Jacqueline
   Information Sheet 9b: Ann
   Information Sheet 9c: L'Arche communities
   Worksheet 9b: research

10. Living With People Around Us
    Information Sheet 10: summary
    Worksheet 10: tasks, including summative poster

THE SHEETS

1 People around us
This section is designed to introduce students to the concept of differences between people and the ways that we judge (and often prejudge) and label people. It might be best to go straight into the worksheet and bring in the pictures at an appropriate point. Alternatively the teacher might make a larger collection of coloured pictures of a wide variety of people to get students talking.

2 Religious Prejudice
This is an extensive area and a very limited selection of examples have been given. There are many more in books and on video. It is good to deal with religious prejudice in more detail in an RE course rather than the usual racial prejudice. Students could select areas which particularly interest them, or be guided by resources available in school. Extra resources are suggested as follows:

- on religious teachings: *Guidelines for Life*, Mel Thompson, Hodder & Stoughton; *Moral Issues in Six Religions*, ed. Owen Cole, Heinemann.
- The Westhill Project series is good for basic beliefs of religions, as is the *World of . . .* series and *Seeking Religion* series by Hodder & Stoughton.
- More information about the Corrymeela community can be obtained from The Corrymeela Community, 8 Upper Crescent, Belfast, BT7 1NT.
- The five books in the *Twelfth Day of July* series by Joan Lingard are an excellent way into the Ulster situation from a positive point of view. Some have been televised.
- The diary of Anne Frank was serialised on BBC TV and is also the theme of a travelling exhibition 'Anne Frank in the World'.

3 Sexual Prejudice
There are many ways that these sheets might be used. A variety of tasks allow students of all abilities to explore this issue. It might be possible to get a visitor in to speak about women's issues in a particular religion, or to arrange for two local ministers to head up the debate about the ordination of women (with differing viewpoints). Students could also be asked to conduct surveys about people's attitudes towards male and female roles, or to look through old (hopefully!) school textbooks for sexist pictures and language. More information on religious teachings can be found in *Moral Issues in Six Religions* (see above).

4 Racial Prejudice
The BBC documentary referred to *Ain't no black in the Union Jack* was made in 1989. To find out more about the CRE, write to Commission for Racial Equality, 10/12 Allington House, London, SW1E 5HE. For less able students the Bible references could be copied out in full and add headings available.

Copyright © 1996 by Sally Lynch. The Publishers grant permission for multiple copies of this page to be made for use solely within that institution.

5 Persecution and Faith in the Past

This section deals with a famous historical example of persecution, and is useful as a starter for discussion. The first task on the worksheet could be tackled as a guided fantasy exercise led by the teacher so that more atmosphere can be generated and hopefully students can begin to think about the issues more clearly. Other areas that this could lead to might be the martyrdom of early Christians or other religious figures. See also: *The Jewish War*, Josephus, Penguin Classics (p385ff for Eleazar's speech); *Oxford Dictionary of Saints* (for early Christian martyrs, e.g. Polycarp, Perpetua and Felicita). Video: *Masada*, MGM, Universal.

6 Persecution Today

This section seeks to introduce students to the work of Amnesty International and to encourage them to see that many people today are persecuted in rather more subtle ways than in the past. It helps them to see how humankind can behave in ways that are inhuman. The BBC each year produces a week's series of short programmes about prisoners of conscience which are a useful introduction to the unit. Examples in the unit are taken from that series. To find out more about Amnesty International, write to 5 Roberts Place, (off Bowling Green Lane), London EC1R 0EJ.

7 Oppression Today

Although it has moved beyond straight oppression into war, the situation in the former Yugoslavia is immediate at the time of writing and something that students can identify with. A little delving in most areas ought to uncover someone who has been or is involved in helping and might come and talk to pupils. It might be worth reading extracts from books written by the British hostages in Lebanon to students as examples of today's less overt oppression.

8 Human Rights

This section aims to encourage students to consider what it is to be human and the basic needs and rights of all people. Task 3 might lead to a discussion of the creation of humankind 'in the image of God' and all 'naked' i.e. with the same starting point. Specific religious teachings might be discussed such as, in Christianity, Genesis 2:26 and Mark 12:31. The sheets are deliberately arranged to allow students to consider their own list of rights before contemplating the UN list and thus being distracted from thinking for themselves.

9 Handicap

This section provides a variety of material for students to use as a base for exploring all types of handicap. The initial worksheet is designed to gauge their first reactions and then to lead to exploration of the issues. Jacqueline and Ann are real people and I am grateful to them for their honesty and bravery in speaking about their handicaps. To find out more about L'Arche, write to L'Arche Secretariat, 14 London Road, Beccles, Suffolk, NR34 9NH. There are also several other communities in Britain which could be contacted. More written information can be found in: *Leading the Way 1*, Mel Thompson, Hodder & Stoughton and also in *Examining Religions, Christianity*, J. Jenkins, Heinemann. The local telephone directory will provide lots of local organisations and branches of national organisations to contact for further research. The film *The Elephant Man* provides lots of discussion material about attitudes towards the handicapped in the past, some of which are still prevalent today.

A useful TV programme, if it can be obtained, is *Julia's Story*, in the 'True Lives' series, Channel 4, 1994. It is about a deaf-blind girl who has a baby, and the first few weeks of coping with help (or otherwise) from social services.

10 Living With People Around Us

This final section aims to help students to think back to all that has been covered in the unit and to consider ways in which they can live with the people around them.

WORDLIST

People Around Us in the Community

This list will help you with the spellings and meanings of key words in this unit.

Denomination
a subsection of a religion – one type of that religion

Discrimination
treating someone less favourably than others because of certain things about them

Exile
being forced to live in another country for some time

Herd Instinct
sticking with people like oneself

Gentiles
non-Jews

Ghetto
an area where people live who are all the same in some way

Infringement
to break a law or rule

Nationalist
being very loyal to one's country

Oppression
to put people down, often for no reason

Persecution
treating someone badly for no apparent reason

Prejudice
making a judgement about someone (usually negative) before getting to know them

Refugee
someone who has had to flee from their country and live in another, not their own

Samaritans
group of Jews of mixed race living in the middle area of Israel

Scapegoat
someone who is made to take the blame for something

Sectarian
smaller groups within one large group

Stereotype
a way of portraying all things that are alike in the same way

Suffragettes
group of women who actively campaigned for women's rights at the start of the twentieth century

Treachery
to betray trust

INFORMATION SHEET 1

PEOPLE AROUND US IN THE COMMUNITY
People Around Us

We live in a number of communities – family, local, national and international. There are many different people who make up these communities. Each of them may be different to us in some way. Some of these ways are quite subtle, others are more obvious. Look at these pictures.

WORKSHEET 1

PEOPLE AROUND US IN THE COMMUNITY

People Around Us

1. a) Look at the people around you in your class. List the ways that each of you is like each other, and the ways that you differ. Think about the things that you can see and the hidden things such as background or beliefs.

   b) What have you found out about the people immediately around you?

2. a) Now think about the people around you in society. Look at the pictures on the information sheet.

   b) In pairs discuss each picture and decide what it is that makes each person individual and different.

   c) Now compare your lists around the class and see if you agree with each other. What did you find out?

   d) Which of the people in the pictures do you like, and which do you dislike? Why?

   (e) Can we really make decisions about people without having met them and got to know them?

3. a) Discuss how we classify people into groups and then list all of the types of groups that we sort people into.

   b) Do you agree with these groupings?

4. On your own complete the following questionnaire:

   > a) How would you feel if you were meeting someone who:
   > - Is older than you?
   > - Is very rich?
   > - Is a different colour to you?
   > - Is handicapped?
   > - Is younger than you?
   > - Is homeless?
   > - Is from a different country?
   >
   > b) Do you agree with the statement 'All people are equal'? Give reasons for your answer.
   >
   > c) Do you think that society treats all people equally? Should it?
   >
   > d) Can you think of any times when you have been treated unfairly or differently?
   >
   > e) Have seen someone else being treated unfairly just because of who or what you are?

   If you wish, share your responses with a small group.

5. Having considered the issues on this sheet, are you now more aware of your own prejudices?

INFORMATION SHEET 2a

PEOPLE AROUND US IN THE COMMUNITY
Religious Prejudice

Religion is one of those topics that people often try not to talk about because it can be very controversial. People's religious beliefs are at the very heart of their being and therefore they can become very uptight when those beliefs are questioned. Likewise, it is sometimes difficult to understand different religious beliefs from our own and so we might say that those who are different are wrong.

Throughout history such ways of seeing things have led to religious persecution – people treating others less favourably, and often with violence, because their religious beliefs differ.

JUDAISM

A notorious example of religious prejudice was the persecution of the Jews by the Nazis before and during World War II. Hitler used Jews as scapegoats for problems in his society and saw them as aliens who did not fit into the 'Aryan Master race'. Jews all over Europe were persecuted and 6 million died in the Nazi death camps. There are many accounts of their sufferings and the inhumane ways that they were treated: wearing a yellow star to distinguish them from other people, having property confiscated, being forced to live in ghettoes and, finally, the most appalling deaths.

Yet persecution of the Jewish race goes back much further than Nazi Germany. In the Middle Ages there was much persecution of the Jews in Britain. They were treated as outcasts and despised, especially those with wealth. The persecution came to a head one Easter when a boy in Norwich was murdered and the Jews were blamed. It was seen as a mockery of the death of Christ. From then on things got worse for Jews and the trouble spread across all of Europe. In York many were burned alive in the castle where they had fled for protection. Many of those who survived were forced to give up their faith and be baptised as Christians.

In modern Israel there are those who would say that the Jewish government has been the persecutor itself in the way that the Palestinian peoples have been treated. Although there are now moves to make peace and share the land, for many years the Palestinian areas were kept in poverty and services were inferior to the Jewish ones.

INFORMATION SHEET 2b

PEOPLE AROUND US IN THE COMMUNITY

Religious Prejudice

SAMARITANS

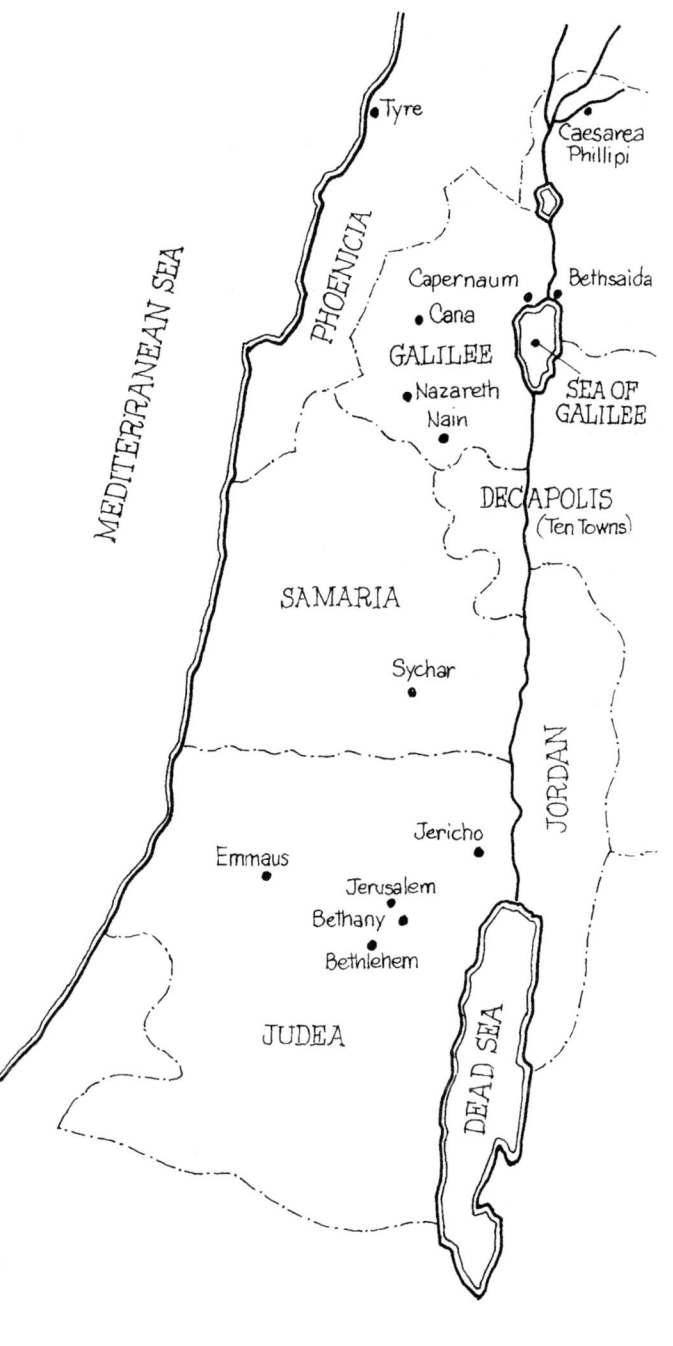

Way back in Bible times the Jews and Samaritans disliked each other. Whenever each came into contact with the other there was often conflict. We can see an example of this in the stories of Jesus. On one occasion Jesus and his disciples were on their way to Jerusalem from Galilee. In order to get there they chose to go through Samaria rather than the usual route which skirted around that area. As Jesus' messengers went ahead of him, the people of a village made it clear that they would not accept Jesus because he was Jewish. The disciples wanted to call down fire from heaven to destroy the Samaritans. Yet Jesus refused, he did not follow the normal Jewish attitudes of the time. He even went on to tell a story about a good Samaritan, one which would have amazed his listeners. (You can read these stories in Luke 9:51-56 and Luke 10:25-37.)

This instance of prejudice goes back to Old Testament times. The tiny country of Israel was often annexed by the bigger superpowers of the time. There were three main areas of Israel: Galilee in the far north, Samaria (often called Israel) in the middle, and Judah (holding the capital, Jerusalem) in the south. In 721 BCE the superpower of Assyria captured the kingdom of Samaria and took the leading Jews back to Assyria. Assyrians were put in charge of Samaria. Over the years these people mixed with the Jews and they inter-married, thus producing a mixed race. These peoples considered themselves Jews and followed the laws of Moses.

In 586 BCE the kingdom of Judah fell to the new Babylonian superpower. Many people were taken to Babylon to live in exile. These people remained 'pure' and would not marry foreigners. When they were able to return to their own land in 520 BCE they looked down on the Samaritans as impure and inferior. A division had arisen which would never be wiped out. Even today the Samaritan people live separately from other Jews in Israel and have their own Torah scrolls.

Copyright © 1996 by Sally Lynch. The Publishers grant permission for multiple copies of this page to be made for use solely within that institution.

PEOPLE AROUND US IN THE COMMUNITY
Religious Prejudice

NORTHERN IRELAND

Many people see the troubles in Ulster (Northern Ireland) as simply religious arguments. In some ways they are correct. In other ways the problem is far more deep-rooted. Religion does play a part because the two 'sides' of the argument can be divided by religion. In fact, Catholic and Protestant are denominations of one religion, Christianity.

Yet the origin of the conflict is, as often, more to do with power and land. In 1169 CE the English king claimed the right to rule Ireland and over the following centuries increasingly strong methods were used to force English rule in Ireland. The new rulers were Protestants from England, while the native people followed the Roman Catholic tradition. Rebellions were put down ruthlessly. In 1800 Britain and Ireland were united, by force. In the second half of the nineteenth century demands for 'Home Rule', that is, self-government for all of Ireland, grew. The Protestants in Ulster wanted to remain part of the United Kingdom. In 1920 Ireland was split into Northern and Southern Ireland (now called Eire and totally independent) while Ulster remains part of the United Kingdom. The IRA and other Republicans want to see the land returned to Irish rule, and are prepared to use violence to make their point. In return, the Protestants wish to remain British, and are also prepared to use violence. In the view of many people, the British Government's action of using troops in order to keep law and order, only worsened the conflict.

Sectarian killings, bombs and booby traps were a part of the way of life for those living in Ulster for almost 25 years. Protestant and Catholic traditionally do not mix. Even the towns are divided into separate areas of housing. David was the Presbyterian (Protestant) minister of a church in Belfast. In 1981 the Roman Catholic church across the road was bombed. He offered the congregation his church building to worship in while theirs was being rebuilt. This angered his own congregation. When the new Roman Catholic church was dedicated, David was invited. He received a warning that he should not go. He got many death threats and his home was attacked because of the friendship that he showed to the 'other side'. In the end he fled from Ulster to live in England so that his family would be safe. He retrained as a priest in the Church of England. On the day that he was instituted in his own parish a number of friends from Ulster were invited. The death threats had continued and the police had to use dogs to check the church before the service. David continues to preach about the need for reconciliation between Christian brothers and sisters in Ulster, and on the mainland.

Yet there is a real hope of peace. On 31 August 1994 the IRA declared a cease-fire. On 13 October the Unionists declared a cease-fire. The politicians have spent long hours talking through the means to an achievable settlement acceptable to most people. There have been many setbacks and much debate with neither side wanting to actually give away too much ground. Yet at the time of writing this book the peace process is well under way through public pressure; an example of how prejudice can be overcome, with lots of effort and real desire to make it work. A teacher in an integrated (joint Catholic/Protestant) school in Northern Ireland wrote:

'We are all too aware that the ending of violence does not necessarily mean the coming of peace. However, it has created a completely new atmosphere within which to carry on our work. It provides fresh impetus for people to get up and do something. It allows some, who might otherwise have been too afraid, to begin to take steps towards "the other side".'

INFORMATION SHEET 2d

PEOPLE AROUND US IN THE COMMUNITY
Religious Prejudice

THE BA'HAI

Many people have not heard of the Ba'hai religion. Yet it is the largest non-Muslim religious community in Iran – and Ba'hai's are widely persecuted there. Ba'hai's believe that all religions teach about one God and they accept the teachings of all prophets such as Moses, Jesus, Muhammad, and Buddha. They believe that Baha'u'llah was the messenger for this age and that another will come in a thousand years. Ba'hai's have been treated very badly in their homeland because they do not conform to the ways of Islam, and many have tried to escape to the West.

Mahmut was born in Russia in 1906. His family had fled there from Iran after his grandfather was killed. Times were also bad in Russia because no religions were allowed under communist rule. His father was arrested on a charge of spying, and sent to prison for six months where he was forced to kneel on gravel among other things. In 1937 the family left Russia and returned to Iran. They were treated as third-class citizens and called names such as 'communist immigrants'.

After the Revolution in 1979 Ba'hai's were openly persecuted. Mahmut owned a big factory by this time, but it was taken over by the government and his children were not allowed to go to school. Food was rationed across the country but ration books were obtained from the mosques and so Ba'hai's had to buy their food on the black market. In the same year Mahmut discovered that his name was on a 'black list' and so he left everything behind – home, family and possessions and managed to get on one of the last planes out to England. His son, who remained in Iran, worked as a doctor and had a very difficult time. When Mahmut arrived in England he had nothing and had to start building his life again.

PEOPLE AROUND US IN THE COMMUNITY
Religious Prejudice

RELIGIOUS TEACHINGS

All religions have teachings about minorities and about relationships with those who are different, or of other faiths. These differ according to the religion, although there is a general concern for justice and peacefulness and for the dignity of human beings as created by God.

JUDAISM

In the Torah there is a concern for minority groups (see Leviticus 19:9-10; 33-34). When Jews refer to their race as the 'chosen' one, it does not mean that Jews are any more important than others, but simply that they have been chosen by God for additional responsibilities. They do not believe that there is a single religion that all should follow, but they look forward to a time when all people will worship that same God. The Talmud even looks to a time when 'there will be neither jealousy, hatred or rivalry'.

CHRISTIANITY

Christians believe that humans were created in the image of God. They do not mean that we look like God, but that we have the same characteristics – we can be loving, caring etc. This means that each human being has dignity and worth, and should thus be treated as of equal value to others. St Paul reminded Christians in the early church that Jesus had emphasised this equality (see Galatians 3:28).

ISLAM

Muslims believe in the unity and equality of the Ummah – the community or family of Islam. All Muslims are equal and should be treated so. When it comes to other faiths, Christianity and Judaism are treated with respect because they also believe in one God, and Muslims accept Moses and Jesus as prophets. Yet Muslims are not expected to mix with those who have no sympathy with their faith. They are expected to take direct action in situations where wrong happens and this might lead to conflict with those of different faiths or those with no faith.

HINDUISM

Hinduism is well known for its caste system, which allows different peoples within one religion to be treated as inferior and superior. This prejudice within the religion leads to some conflict, yet it is also clear that the different castes and peoples are interdependent and thus each person should live their own life. When it comes to other faiths, Hindus and Muslims are in conflict in India because of their different religious beliefs. However, this is not the case in Britain. There are two Hindu traditions concerning the use of violence, one of which teaches that it should never be used, and the other that it is permissible in certain necessary circumstances. On the whole Hinduism tolerates other faiths.

SIKHISM

Sikhism teaches that all people are equal and that discrimination on any grounds is wrong. All people are treated equally by Sikhs, and anyone may eat in the Sikh langar. Guru Nanak taught that the caste system was wrong, and this has lead to some conflict between Sikhs and Hindus in India, although it does not normally affect relations in Britain.

BUDDHISM

Buddhists believe that humankind's problems are of our own making and that they stem from wrong attitudes in the minds of people. They teach that all people deserve equal respect, and that humans should make an effort to see themselves as equal to others. To do this they have to balance the love they have for themselves with the love they have for others. Buddhists teach that they should practise loving-kindness towards all people and that this will prevent prejudice and division.

We have seen what each religion teaches about relationships with others. Yet it is often the more specific teachings of a religion that can be the cause of conflict – either intentionally when a group pick on someone of another faith because of their beliefs, or unintentionally when someone expects a person to do something that they cannot because of the teachings of their faith.

WORKSHEET 2

PEOPLE AROUND US IN THE COMMUNITY
Religious Prejudice

Attempt some of these tasks using the information sheets about religious prejudice.

1. Choose one of the examples given. Imagine that you are a follower of that faith. Write a diary which shows how prejudice has affected that particular religion (or denomination).

2. Write an article for a newspaper or magazine explaining what religious prejudice is and giving examples. Suggest how it might be prevented.

3. Use one of the examples given, or choose your own (real or imaginary). Draw a cartoon strip to tell a story about the prejudice which affects your example.

4. Look at the information about religious teachings. In a small group discuss what each says. How do you relate these to the examples given?

5. Prepare notes and hold a debate on the motion: This house believes that religious people are the most prejudiced of all people.

You will need to use resources to research further in these tasks.

6. a) Find out more about the teachings of one or more religion on prejudice and relations with others.
   b) Discuss your findings with a partner.
   c) Produce an information leaflet about these teachings.

7. Imagine that you have a friend coming to stay who is a Muslim or a Jew. Find out about Muslim or Jewish beliefs and write about the special preparations that you will have to make in order to make sure that his/her stay is acceptable. Think about what you will eat, what you will do, and so on.

8. Imagine that you are an employer who has recently taken on a number of Sikh or Buddhist workers. Find out about Sikh or Buddhist beliefs and write about the arrangements that you will need to make so that they will not be asked to compromise their beliefs at work.

9. Find out more about the Jewish Holocaust and modern memorials to it such as Yad Vashem in Jerusalem. What memorial might you build for such mass discrimination? Read *The Diary of Anne Frank*.

10. Find out about efforts for peace and religious harmony in Ulster. There are over twenty schools specially opened for Catholic and Protestant children and the Corrymeela community seeks to bring unity between the two 'sides'. Read the series of books *The Twelfth Day of July*.

11. Find out about the Ecumenical movement in the Christian church. Design a poster which explains what it is, and how it might help to prevent prejudice between Christians.

12. Using all that you have found out in this section, write a poem, or design a poster, about religious prejudice or discrimination.

INFORMATION SHEET 3

PEOPLE AROUND US IN THE COMMUNITY

Sexual Prejudice

Karen is 34. She has a good honours degree in Engineering from Oxford University. She works for a reputable firm of engineers designing fuel efficient systems for small cars. She applied for a senior post in the firm that became available, and despite her long service and good qualifications, she did not get the job. It went to a less well-qualified man. She felt that she had been discriminated against.

Sandra is 16 and has just left school. She loves cars and has always enjoyed messing about with the family car. She has learned a lot about them, and wanted to work as a car mechanic. After a lot of searching she managed to get a job in a garage not too far from home. When she started work she found that all she was allowed to do was to work the petrol pump and make the tea. She is about to complain to the boss.

Tony is 28 and a nurse. He has completed all of his training and passed his exams with flying colours. He enjoys working with babies and feels proud that he can help a couple to bring a new life into the world. He has decided to become a midwife. One of his first patients became very unpleasant and refused to be 'looked after by a man'. Now he is not sure whether to continue his midwifery training or to go into another field of nursing.

There are many jobs that are seen as being for men or women only. Yet many people today claim that men and women should be equal in the world of work and life in general. Life has certainly changed for women over the past century. They are now able to vote, stand for Parliament, own property, divorce their husbands and to choose whether or not to marry and have children. Laws have been passed in Britain which make it illegal to discriminate against people in many areas of life, and particularly in employment, on grounds of their sex.

Obviously there are physical differences between men and women. Traditionally men have been seen as the hunters or breadwinners and women as the homemakers and 'breeders'. These roles have begun to change, especially with the Suffragette movement earlier this century. Better methods of family planning mean that women do not have to simply be 'baby machines' and different attitudes have meant that wider roles are available for women in public life.

In schools the old stereotypes found in textbooks and pictures have disappeared, and equal opportunities exist in all subject areas.

Technology is open to all pupils, it is no longer girls doing cookery and boys doing woodwork. In the media, the images of women have changed, although the glamour girl is still used in some advertising, alongside sexy men!

Religions are sometimes accused of being old fashioned in their attitudes towards the sexes. Some are mistaken as seeing women as inferior. In fact all religions see different and complimentary roles for men and women which pick up on their natural physical differences. The Buddha taught that it was just as possible for women to become enlightened as it was for men. Hindu attitudes are changing in recent years, although there is still male dominance. A Hindu woman may be well educated but she may not become a priest and there are still a number of restrictions on her married and religious life.

Despite the popular media image in Britain, Islam actually teaches that men and women are equal before Allah. Both have the same spiritual worth and rights. The physical differences are recognised in the rights that are given to women – protection, modest dress and to be provided for by their husbands.

Judaism also teaches that men and women are equal before God, but sees marriage and motherhood as vital to a woman's fulfilling of her faith and being. Women are excused some religious duties so that they can fulfil this aim well.

Within Sikhism there is the same teaching of equality and women may perform any religious duty or hold office in the Sikh community.

Christianity is often portrayed as sexist with an emphasis on the male role, especially in worship. This was the case in the past and is now beginning to change, but with fierce debate. Yet Jesus himself was very open in his outlook and treated the women of his own day with far more freedom than was usual. He emphasised respect for the female role in the community.

WORKSHEET 3

PEOPLE AROUND US IN THE COMMUNITY
Sexual Prejudice

1. Look at the case studies.
   a) Do you think that this sort of thing really happens in Britain?
   b) Do you think that there are some jobs that are just for men and some just for women?

2. a) List the differences between men and women.
   b) Which are 'real', and which are 'man-made'?

3. Find out how life has changed for women in this century.

4. Prepare notes and hold a debate on the motion: This house believes that a woman's place is in the home.

5. In a group role play these situations (add characters as you need them)

   A) You are a building firm. A new employee has started work – it is a girl. How does her first day go?
   Characters:
   Girl
   the Boss
   several male workers
   (Your views vary, some agree with her being there, some don't.)

   B) You are a maternity hospital. One of your best midwives is male. One day an expectant mother comes in who refuses to have her baby delivered by a man. What happens?
   Characters:
   Expectant mother and father
   male midwife
   female midwife
   consultant
   another mother

   C) You are a top-class firm of lawyers, holding interviews for a partnership in the firm. One of the interviewees is a highly qualified young woman with three children. The others are all single, or married men. How does it go?
   Characters:
   female interviewee
   three male interviewees
   two male interviewers
   female secretary.

6. a) Look at the information about religions and sexism. Discuss the different teachings in a group.
   b) Do you agree with each religion?
   Give reasons for your answer.
   c) Find out more about the attitude of one or more religions.

7. Design a poster which shows the variety of attitudes towards male and female roles in religions and society.

8. Prepare notes and hold a debate on the motion: This house believes that the Church of England is right to ordain women as priests.

INFORMATION SHEET 4

PEOPLE AROUND US IN THE COMMUNITY
Racial Prejudice

In 1989 the BBC made a documentary about prejudice in Britain. It aimed to discover whether racial prejudice still exists. Two young reporters spent some time testing out various British institutions. One was black, the other white. In one episode they try to rent a room. The black man is refused lodgings in some places, while the white man is offered a room in the same places. In all, one-third of the bed and breakfast lodgings they tried treated the black reporter less favourably. They concealed a video recorder in their cases to capture the reactions of the people they mixed with. The programmes were called *Ain't no black in the Union Jack* and they showed a disturbing amount of colour prejudice in this country.

Why are people prejudiced against those of other colours or races?

- Fear: often we are afraid of things that are different and our fear turns to self-protection and insults the other person.
- Scapegoating: we need to blame others for the things that go wrong in our lives and in our societies. It is easiest to pick on the minority groups.
- Herd instinct: humans tend to stick with people like themselves. Look at your group of friends, many of them will be like you, sharing interests etc. If you went to live in another country you would probably want to live nearby people like yourself – who spoke your language and held the same customs – and so this works two ways. Races tend to stick together, almost in ghettoes, for comfort, and people then label them as anti-social!
- Jealousy: sometimes we see things that others have that we would like and are jealous. This shows itself by picking on the others and finding things that are their weaknesses or their differences.

Discrimination in any form is illegal in Britain. The 1976 Race Relations Act makes it illegal to discriminate against anyone in the areas of employment, housing, education and provision of goods and services. It covers every area of life. It is an offence to use racist language in public or to stir up racial hatred.

The Commission for Racial Equality was set up to monitor the Act and to provide a place of help for those who believe that they have been discriminated against. It also seeks to educate the public about good race relations.

The Christian church teaches that all kinds of racism are wrong – all people are the same to God. Some churches in areas of high immigrant population have tried to set up centres to help all peoples to mix together freely and in peace. Other religious groups have also set up similar projects to help people of different races to get along together.

WORKSHEET 4

PEOPLE AROUND US IN THE COMMUNITY

Racial Prejudice

1. Imagine that you were the reporters in the BBC documentary film. Write your newspaper report once your research was over.

2. Find out about an incident of racial prejudice in Britain. Draw a cartoon strip of the story. Suggest what solution might be reached and how.

3. Look up and read the following passages in the Bible and match each one up to what it teaches about racial prejudice. One has been done for you.

4. Find out about the work of the Commission for Racial Equality. Is there a branch nearby that could send someone along to talk to your class?

5. Design a poster to help different races get along together – try to include some religious teachings too.

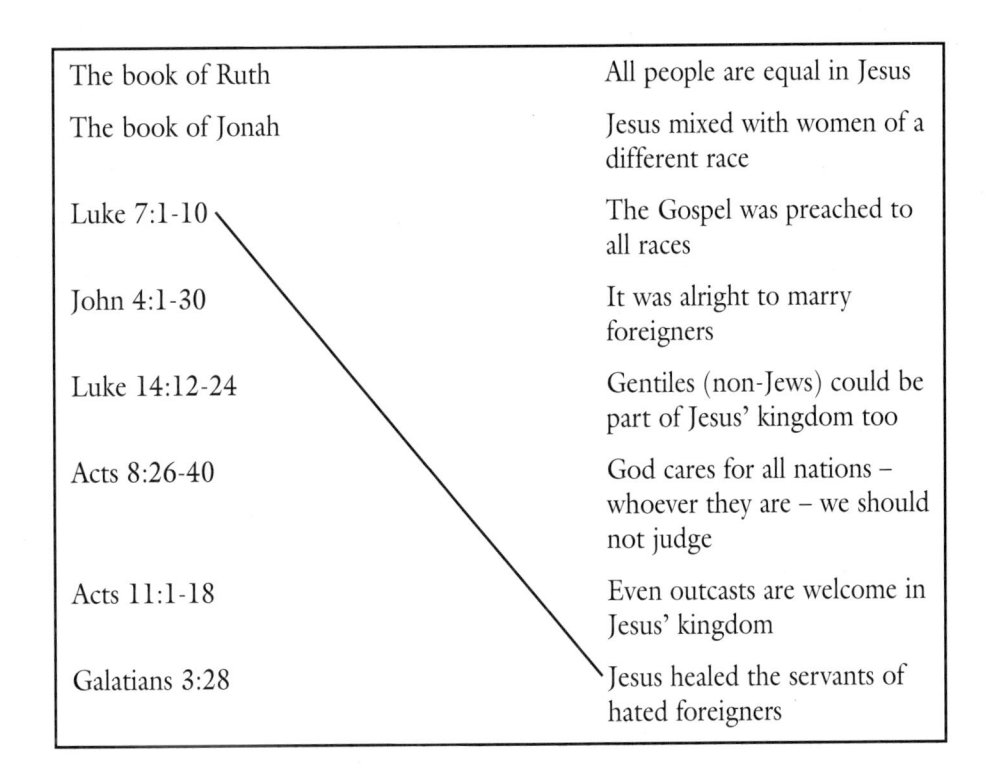

The book of Ruth	All people are equal in Jesus
The book of Jonah	Jesus mixed with women of a different race
Luke 7:1-10	The Gospel was preached to all races
John 4:1-30	It was alright to marry foreigners
Luke 14:12-24	Gentiles (non-Jews) could be part of Jesus' kingdom too
Acts 8:26-40	God cares for all nations – whoever they are – we should not judge
Acts 11:1-18	Even outcasts are welcome in Jesus' kingdom
Galatians 3:28	Jesus healed the servants of hated foreigners

(Luke 7:1-10 is matched to "Jesus healed the servants of hated foreigners")

Copyright © 1996 by Sally Lynch. The Publishers grant permission for multiple copies of this page to be made for use solely within that institution.

INFORMATION SHEET 5a

PEOPLE AROUND US IN THE COMMUNITY
Persecution and Faith in the Past

At the time of Jesus, the country of Israel was occupied by the Romans. This upset the Jews because they believed that God had chosen them to be his special people and given them the land as their own. The Romans flouted Jewish laws and forced heavy taxes from the people. Some Jews, known as Zealots, revolted, but were regularly put down by the soldiers. The Zealots were radical nationalists and even willing to kill Romans. They looked forward to the coming of a Messiah who would lead them to victory against the Romans and fulfil their scriptures. In 66 CE the Jews revolted for the last time. Many Jews were killed. Jerusalem fell and the Temple was destroyed in 70 CE.

Masada is a huge rocky plateau in the desert south of Jerusalem. The only way to the top then was by a narrow footpath. At the start of the rebellion some of the Zealots had taken over Masada, and they were later joined by other Jewish families fleeing Jerusalem.

The Jews were led by Eleazar ben Ya'ir, as they defended the rock, and their faith, from the Roman armies below. They adapted the palaces which King Herod had built on the rock and made living quarters and command posts. They had a synagogue and good water supply on top of Masada. They had all that they needed to live, except their freedom.

After Jerusalem fell, the Romans, under the command of General Silva, were determined to capture Masada and the Jews living there. It took them many months to construct a ramp, so that they could use a battering ram and take the fortress. The Jews had the advantage of height and good supplies, but in 73 CE the walls were eventually breached and Masada fell.

When the Romans reached the top their victory was hollow. They found plentiful supplies of food, weapons and goods. But every Jew was dead – killed by their own hands rather than face slavery and loss of their faith and identity under the Romans.

WORKSHEET 5

PEOPLE AROUND US IN THE COMMUNITY

Persecution and Faith in the Past

1. Imagine that you were there at the fall of Masada. Try to take the parts of both Romans and Jews.

    A) You are a Roman soldier. General Silva has kept you working in the desert for months on little water, taunted by the Jews on top of the rock who throw water down at you and who will not give in to the might of Rome. You are greatly relieved when the ramp is complete and you are one of the first through the breach. All you find on the top is death. Suicide!
    How do you feel about the Jews?

    B) You are a Jewish man/woman living on top of Masada. The Romans have completed the ramp. You are frightened. Eleazar has made a powerful speech urging that you commit mass suicide rather than allow yourselves to be taken by the pagan Romans.
    How do you feel about this?
    Choose a way in which to report your reaction to each of the above situations.

2. Read Eleazar's final speech on Information Sheet 5b. Discuss with a partner whether you agree with it.

3. Discuss in groups whether you think that it is ever right that someone should die by execution or by suicide, rather than give up their faith. Is there a difference between execution and suicide in such cases?

4. Can you think of any people who might be in similar, perhaps less dramatic, situations today? (e.g. someone at your school who goes to church or who keeps the five pillars of the Muslim faith, and will not stop, despite teasing from others.) Is there anything that you or your class could do about it?

5. a) What sort of things do people today really care about?
   b) What do you really care about?
   c) Is there anything that you would not be prepared to give up – even to the point of death?
   d) Try to write your own speech (or tape record one) like the final speech of Eleazar, which sums up why this thing is so important to you.

INFORMATION SHEET 5b

PEOPLE AROUND US IN THE COMMUNITY

Persecution and Faith in the Past

Eleazar's Speech

'My loyal followers, long ago we resolved to serve neither the Romans nor anyone else but only God, who alone is the true and righteous Lord of men: now the time has come that bids us prove our determination by our deeds. At such a time we must not disgrace ourselves: hitherto we have never submitted to slavery, even when it brought no danger with it: we must not choose slavery now, and with it penalties that will mean the end of everything if we fall alive into the hands of the Romans. For we were the first of all to revolt, and shall be the last to break off the struggle. And I think it is God who has given us this privilege, that we can die nobly and as free men, unlike others who were unexpectedly defeated. In our case it is evident that daybreak will end our resistance, but we are free to choose an honourable death with our loved ones. This our enemies cannot prevent, however earnestly they may pray to take us alive; nor can we defeat them in battle.

'From the very first, when we were bent on claiming our freedom but suffered such constant misery at each other's hands and worse at the enemy's, we ought perhaps to have read the mind of God and realized that His once beloved Jewish race had been sentenced to extinction. For if He had remained gracious or only slightly indignant with us, He would not have shut His eyes to the destruction of so many thousands or allowed His most holy City to be burnt to the ground by our enemies. We hoped, or so it would seem, that of all of the Jewish race we alone would come through safe, still in possession of our freedom, as if we had committed no sin against God and taken part in no crime – we who had taught the others! Now see how He shows the folly of our hopes, plunging us into miseries more terrible than any we had dreamt of. Not even the impregnability of our fortress has sufficed to save us, but though we have food in abundance, ample supplies of arms, and more than enough of every other requisite, God Himself without a doubt has taken away all hope of survival. The fire that was being carried into the enemy lines did not turn back of its own accord towards the wall we had built: these things are God's vengeance for the many wrongs that in our madness we dared to do to our own countrymen.

'For those wrongs let us pay the penalty not to our bitterest enemies, the Romans, but to God – by our own hands. It will be easier to bear. Let our wives die unabused, our children without knowledge of slavery: after that, let us do each other an ungrudging kindness, preserving our freedom as a glorious winding-sheet. But first let our possessions and the whole fortress go up in flames: it will be a bitter blow to the Romans, that I know, to find our persons beyond their reach and nothing left for them to loot. One thing only let us spare – our store of food: it will bear witness when we are dead to the fact that we perished, not through want but because, as we resolved at the beginning, we chose death rather than slavery.

'We were very proud of our courage, so we revolted from Rome: now in the final stages they have offered to spare our lives and we have turned the offer down. Is anyone too blind to see how furious they will be if they take us alive? Pity the young whose bodies are strong enough to survive prolonged torture; pity the not-so-young whose old frames would break under such ill-usage. A man will see his wife violently carried off; he will hear the voice of his child crying "Daddy!" when his own hands are fettered. Come! while our hands are free and can hold a sword, let them do a noble service! Let us die unenslaved by our enemies, and leave this world as free men in company with our wives and children. That is what the Law ordains, that is what our wives and children demand of us, the necessity God has laid on us, the opposite of what the Romans wish – they are anxious none of us should die before the town is captured. So let us deny the enemy their hoped-for pleasure at our expense, and without more ado leave them to be dumbfounded by our death and awed by our courage.'

INFORMATION SHEET 6

PEOPLE AROUND US IN THE COMMUNITY

Persecution Today

We have seen in other sections that people have been persecuted for various reasons in the recent and more distant past. But are people still persecuted today?

Unfortunately people are, although it is perhaps more subtle these days. There may be people in our own country who are persecuted because of what they believe in, from a very simple form of bullying at school because they follow a religion, through to more unpleasant treatment of older people because they are prepared to stand up for things which are important to them.

The situation is often far worse for some people in Developing or Eastern Countries. Where people are prepared to speak out against injustice or against the State they are often punished in some way – quite severely. These people are often called 'prisoners of conscience'.

Dr Ushari Mahmood was a lecturer in languages at the University of Khartoum. He has two sons. He was well known for his human rights work and a good teacher with a sense of humour. In May 1987 he heard rumours of a massacre of Dinka people in Sudan. He investigated and found that over 1000 people had been killed in appalling ways, with many women and children being taken as slaves. He wrote a report blaming the Sudanese Government for covering up the massacre, and actually being behind it. He called for an investigation. In Sudan, criticising the government is seen as treachery and he was arrested twice, questioned, and released. After a military coup in Sudan he was again arrested and sent to jail because the new military government wanted to get rid of trouble makers.

Andreas Christodoulou is a Jehovah's Witness. In Greece, where he lives, all men between 18 and 40 may be called up to serve in the army for about 20 months. Andreas's faith means that he cannot fight and so when he received his call-up papers he refused to join and was sent to prison for four years. He is allowed only one family visitor but no leader of the Jehovah's Witnesses may visit him. There are many other young men like him in Greek prisons.

Many people in the West are concerned about such treatment and want to do something about it. In 1961 an organisation was started by a British lawyer to do something about the way that people were being illegally treated and imprisoned throughout the world. From small beginnings Amnesty International has grown so that today it has over 500,000 volunteer workers in 160 different countries.

Amnesty International is not a political, religious or government organisation. It is simply concerned for anyone who suffers abuse at the hands of others. The three aims of Amnesty are:
- to seek the release of all prisoners of conscience;
- to ask for fair and prompt trials for all political prisoners and for people being detained without charge or trial;
- to oppose the death penalty and torture for all prisoners.

Amnesty investigates cases of prisoners of conscience and publishes reports on ways that people are being mistreated. There are about 300 local Amnesty groups and these 'adopt' prisoners. The group appeals to the relevant government and anyone else who might be able to help their person. Letter writing is a key means of trying to achieve release for these people. Letters are always short, courteous and relevant, they aim to put pressure on the governments. Funds are also raised to help the prisoners or their families. Sometimes there are urgent appeals for help if a need arises, such as a disappearance or torture. Local groups send letters, telexes and telegrams to try to prevent execution or torture.

Amnesty International also has a network of school groups and young people in this country who are keen to support the work.

WORKSHEET 6

PEOPLE AROUND US IN THE COMMUNITY
Persecution Today

1. Look at these sayings and discuss each in a small group. How might they relate to situations of persecution today?

> Sticks and stones may break my bones, but words will never hurt me.
>
> *School boy*

> In fact, everyone who wants to live a godly life in Christ Jesus will be persecuted, ...
>
> *St Paul (2 Timothy 3:12)*

> ... long ago we resolved to serve only God ... we must not disgrace ourselves ... we must not choose slavery now ... God has given us the privilege to die as free men ...
>
> *Eleazar Ben Ya'ir*

> Blessed are those who are persecuted because of righteousness, for theirs is the Kingdom of Heaven.
>
> *Jesus (Matthew 5:10)*

2. Write a newspaper article, or make a taped report, about a prisoner of conscience to make other people aware of his/her plight. Include:
   - what he/she is said to have done;
   - what has happened to him/her;
   - the effect on his/her family;
   - what the future seems to hold for him/her.

3. Now write two letters or postcards. One to the person that you wrote about in task 2, to encourage them that they are not forgotten. The second to the Government of that country, putting the case for release of your person. Remember to be tactful.

4. You might want to find out more about the work of Amnesty International, and perhaps even to set up a group in school.

5. Design a poster which explains the work of Amnesty International, and especially suggests how young people in Britain might get involved with its work.

6. Look at the Amnesty International symbol below and try to explain what it shows. Is it appropriate? Could you think of another one?

INFORMATION SHEET 7

PEOPLE AROUND US IN THE COMMUNITY
Oppression Today

Oppression is when one group treats another group badly for no apparent reason. There are examples of oppression all over the world. In South Africa the black majority of the population were oppressed by the white minority for some years and treated badly. This has now changed. In some countries of South America the poor people are being oppressed and deliberately kept poor by their governments – it is easier to keep control of people who are poor. Those who speak out, including a number of Roman Catholic priests, are killed or badly treated. Many 'disappear'.

Wars often result from oppression. In 1992 civil war broke out in Yugoslavia. The country was made up of a number of states and each of these declared independence when Tito, the dictator who had ruled them as a group of communist states, died. Each state was characterised by different ethnic groups – Muslims, Serbs and Croats. The stronger of these groups treated the weaker groups very badly. Many ancient and beautiful cities were ruined and whole villages destroyed in the fighting that followed. Thousands of people lost their lives both in the fighting forces and as innocent civilians. The way of life was reduced to scrabbling for a living on what remained of their countries.

Many people throughout the rest of the world decided that while the politicians on all sides were arguing out the situation, something needed to be done for the millions of ordinary people for whom life had changed in the space of months. Many had no home, little food, clothing or possessions left. Medical services and supplies were appalling. Soldiers sent in by the United Nations to attempt to ease the situation for such folk talked about sorts of torture that they had never seen before. The oppression became widespread amongst both sides. One soldier said 'whichever part of the country you go to, there is always an underdog'. The weakest suffered.

Some people in the West helped by raising money and trying to send aid. Some organised buses to take out food, clothing and basic necessities. Many ordinary people, especially in the state of Bosnia, had become refugees and lost almost all that they owned. A few were also taken back on the buses' return trips and looked after in special centres set up in Britain and parts of Europe. Here they were given hope for future and some even settled in the new country.

In 1994 a similar situation erupted in the African state of Rwanda. Again many people became refugees, millions of others simply died. Aid agencies were swamped with needy people and again there were collections to raise money to help in the West.

Oppression may also occur; for no apparent reason to individuals. Between 1986 and 1992 three British men, Brian Keenan, John McCarthy and Terry Waite, were kidnapped and held hostage by terrorist groups in Lebanon. These groups held other Europeans and Americans as hostages too. The way that each was treated during their captivity was simple oppression – no fresh air, little food, usually being chained to a wall by their feet, and wearing a blindfold when in the presence of their kidnappers.

WORKSHEET 7

PEOPLE AROUND US IN THE COMMUNITY
Oppression Today

1. Imagine that you are running a centre in Britain which will take in 20 refugees from the Bosnian Republic. In pairs, make two lists of the things that you will need to prepare for their arrival:
   - physical and material needs;
   - emotional and spiritual needs.

2. Look at these pictures and suggest how, why and by whom, these people are being oppressed.

3. Find out more about what happened to one of the three British hostages in Lebanon. Make a list of the things that happened to them that you would call oppression.

4. Prepare notes and debate the following:
   This house believes that there is no oppression in Britain today.

WORKSHEET 8

PEOPLE AROUND US IN THE COMMUNITY
Human Rights

'It's not fair. I wasn't doin' nothing, and I just got arrested.'

'... and then my Dad hurt me and he told me not to tell anyone – it's our secret, he said.'

'I'm not at all happy about joining the Union, but they won't employ me there otherwise.'

'But I want to marry Ranjit, we love each other.'

What would you do if someone prevented you from doing something, or being the person that you wanted to be? How many times in the last 24 hours have you said, 'It's not fair'? All of the things that the people above are complaining about might be infringements of their basic human rights.

1a) Make a list of the things that you think all human beings have a right to simply because they are human beings.
b) Compare your list with a partner and produce one list.
c) Now compare this list with another pair and make one list.
d) Keep going until you have a class list of human rights. Discuss why you have arrived at the list you have, and anything that has been missed out along the way.

2a) Now look at the United Nations Universal Declaration of Human Rights (Information Sheet 8). Compare your lists with it.
b) Using the UN Declaration:
(i) Find out the meanings of any words in the list that you do not know.
(ii) Choose the 10 points that you think are most important.
(iii) For each of these try to find a newspaper or magazine article or picture which shows that right being broken (ideally in Britain) today.
(iv) Discuss how you might help people in general to keep this list of rights for themselves and each other.

3 Why do you think that religious people might especially want to support this list of human rights?

INFORMATION SHEET 8

PEOPLE AROUND US IN THE COMMUNITY

Human Rights

The United Nations organisation was set up in 1945 to help and encourage nations throughout the world to support each other and to live in peace together. One of its main principles is that all member countries are equal. Most countries of the world are now members.

In 1948 the UN produced a Universal Declaration of Human Rights which lists those things that the UN believes that all people have a right to, simply because they are human beings.

- All human beings are born free and equal.
- Everyone has the right to life, liberty and freedom from fear and violence.
- Everyone has the right to protection of the law without discrimination.
- No one shall be subjected to arbitrary arrest, detention or exile.
- Everyone has the right to a fair and public trial.
- Everyone charged with a penal offence has the right to be assumed innocent until proved guilty.
- No one shall be subjected to arbitrary interference with his privacy, family, home or correspondence, nor to attacks on his reputation.
- Everyone has the right to freedom of movement within his own country and abroad.
- Everyone has the right to a nationality.
- Adults have the right to marry and found a family regardless of race or religion.
- Both men and women are entitled to equal rights within marriage and in divorce.
- Everyone has the right to own property. No one should be arbitrarily deprived of his property.
- Everyone has the right to freedom of thought, conscience and religion and the right to express their opinion both privately and publicly.
- Everyone has the right to attend meetings and join associations.
- No one should be forced to join an association.
- Everyone has the right to take part in the government of his or her country.
- Everyone has the right to work and to just and favourable conditions of employment.
- Everyone has the right to equal pay for equal work.
- Everyone has the right to fair pay to enable him and his family to live with self-respect.
- Everyone has the right to join a trades union.
- Everyone has the right to rest and leisure, including reasonable working hours and holidays with pay.
- Everyone has the right to a standard of living adequate for their health and well-being, including housing, medical care and social security in the event of unemployment, sickness, widowhood and old age.
- Everyone has the right to an education.
- Everyone has the right to enjoy the cultural life of the community and to share in its scientific advancements and benefits.
- Everyone has duties to the community to ensure the full recognition and respect for the rights and freedom of others.

WORKSHEET 9a

PEOPLE AROUND US IN THE COMMUNITY

Handicap

1. a) What do you think of when you hear the word handicap? In groups brainstorm the word HANDICAP.

   b) Now divide your findings into:
   - types of handicap;
   - descriptions of handicap and its effects;
   - opinions;
   - other comments.

   c) What can you learn about your attitudes in your groups?

2. List all the different types of handicap that you can think of as a class. Does the length of your list surprise you?

3. a) You could try to imagine what it is like to be handicapped. In small groups take it in turns to try the following.

   - Be blindfolded and try to walk around the room or make a cup of tea.
   - Wear headphones playing very loud sounds so that you cannot hear anything else and try to follow a lesson.
   - Tie one arm out of use and try to make a cup of tea or carry books.
   - Read a book in a language which is totally strange to you.

   b) How did it feel to do these things and to watch others doing them?

INFORMATION SHEET 9a

PEOPLE AROUND US IN THE COMMUNITY

Handicap – Jacqueline

Jacqueline is 26. She lives in a house with another woman and two men. They each have their own bedroom, and share a kitchen, lounge, bathroom and laundry. She works at a training centre doing light industrial jobs and once a week she helps at a special school, looking after mentally handicapped toddlers. She helps with a local Brownie pack and goes to the church near her home, where she helps with coffee mornings and is a member of a Bible-study group. She has a boyfriend, and they go to the pub together. Her mother, Edna, says 'I know I can rely on Jacqueline, we've always been good friends'.

Her mother gradually became aware that something was wrong as Jacqueline began to develop as a baby. She was diagnosed as mentally handicapped, but went to a mainstream school when she was 4½ years old. Other children bullied her. She went home and asked her mother what the words meant that they had called her. Her mother told her to ignore them, and she still does. Edna says that it is hard to accept that your child is handicapped, but she believes that it is other people that have missed out when they patronise Jacqueline, as she has so much to give. While Jacqueline was at mainstream school, Edna was called an 'unfit mother' because she fought for her to be transferred to a special school. It was a difficult time for the family too – Jacqueline has an older sister and it was necessary to balance the needs of both of them.

Eventually Edna won her case and Jacqueline was able to attend a special school where she was happy. Yet all was not easy. She was not allowed to join the Brownies – the Guiders could not deal with her handicap; and she was asked to leave Sunday School (the first thing she had been able to do on her own) because the teachers did not know how to cope with an older girl among little children. A lady at church once said to Edna 'She's such a nice girl, it's such a pity she's like she is'.

Then a chance meeting with a different local vicar and his family led to Jacqueline and Edna joining a new church and she was accepted by their Guide company. Jacqueline left school at 16 because they could 'do no more for her' and she went to work at the training centre. She was still living at home, and Edna was worried about what lay in the future. She had fought for Jacqueline all her life and when the place became available at the Partial Support home they were delighted.

The home is run by the Mencap Homes Foundation and means that Jacqueline now has her independence, yet help is always on hand if necessary. The fact that she is able to get involved in so much is a testimony to her mother's support and the care of many people – and her own sheer determination. She has been horse riding for about eight years and won a gold medal at a 'Riding for the Disabled' mini Olympics. Once other people, especially the children she works with, know what is 'wrong' with her they are able to associate with her easily.

Despite her handicap, Jacqueline is able to lead a fun, full life, now independent from her mother; yet sharing her joys with her. Edna says that she feels sorry for people who can't cope with her handicap, 'Other people only see the outside, and never get to know the real person'. Jacqueline's ambition is to work full time at the special school, and to go on a riding holiday. Her mum is proud of her.

INFORMATION SHEET 9b

PEOPLE AROUND US IN THE COMMUNITY

Handicap – Ann

Ann is married with two children. Susan is 16 and Scott is 10. Ann developed polio when she was 1 year old and spent about nine months in hospital. She had just started walking, but she came out of hospital with callipers and has had to wear them ever since. She went to a 'normal' primary school, but found it very difficult to cope with the steps, and so after a short time of home tuition, she was sent to a residential church school for handicapped children. It was a long way from her parents' home, but they visited her as often as they could. When the family moved house, she was able to go to the local primary and then secondary schools.

Whilst at school she got on well with other pupils, who treated her just the same as they were. There was some difficulty with stairs as there were no handrails, but she always found someone to hang on to. She says that she would always urge parents with physically handicapped children to try to get them into a mainstream school. Ann longed to be able to do gym and swimming at school, but the teachers would not let her, for fear of her hurting herself. She made up for this outside school, by climbing trees and walking down to the local swimming baths regularly – even in thick snow, although she could never climb up to the diving board to join in fully. She reckons that her independent personality enabled her to cope. It was also easier to climb trees as her arm muscles were more developed, making up for weakness in her legs. The boys were jealous that she could get higher than them! Today most schools will encourage handicapped youngsters to take a full part in all activities.

She was channelled into secretarial work as it was a 'nice sitting-down job', but walking to work every day, albeit slowly, kept her fit. She got married and moved area a number of times; each time working in hospital or social services administration. She left work when she became pregnant with Susan. She faced some difficulties and frustrations at this time, especially when the car park attendant would not allow her, heavily pregnant to park near the hospital entrance on ante-natal visits. At that time there were no facilities for the disabled. Eventually a 'phone call from her husband to the hospital sorted the matter out. Following a caesarean birth, she helped to set up the first, of what is now, a nationwide network of caesarean support groups. This enabled her to give advice about the needs of people with walking disabilities when a new maternity hospital was built in the area.

Ann believes that facilities for the disabled have improved over recent years and is pleased to see the tightening up of the orange-badge parking scheme – some people were abusing it to get easy parking. She says that you should try going out with a baby buggy and if you can't get that into places, then there will be problems for disabled people. Some shops, for example, still do not have lifts to enable them to get to the higher store levels.

When her own children were small, Ann became a registered childminder and still looks after a number of young children each week. She can be seen riding through the village on a trike, 'I don't have enough strength in the legs for a bike', with a child in the rear seat. She says that she had no difficulty being registered as she had worked for social services and they knew her. The children tend not to notice her handicap. In fact people sometimes forget and ask her to do things that are impossible.

She enjoys walking in the hills, but at her own pace. She doesn't do as much these days, but has always been ready to have a go at things. Experience has taught her to always have a spare calliper in case hers break. This has happened on a number of occasions – sometimes in awkward situations such as on holiday. She has shoes and callipers specially made, and these are supplied by the NHS. She is able to send a design that she has seen for 'normal' shoes and have them made as near to that as possible. Her disability will not get worse, but her daughter Susan says that she wishes her mum didn't have to wear the callipers. Ann is less concerned. She says that she has known nothing else and that other parts of the body compensate for the weakness. 'You find other ways of doing things', she says. So when Susan was a baby she was carried downstairs – backwards!

INFORMATION SHEET 9c

PEOPLE AROUND US IN THE COMMUNITY
L'Arche Communities

Do people care about the handicapped? There are many organisations set up to care for people with various handicaps. These organisations also carry out, or fund, valuable research into the handicap in an attempt to cure, or control, and make life easier for sufferers. They also help to educate the public about the needs of the handicapped. Yet all people need more than this, handicapped or not. They need to be loved and accepted as part of a community. Many handicapped people do not have that security, for a number of reasons.

The L'Arche communities are just one example of a group set up by people who care, sometimes sparked off by their religious faith, and who want to make handicapped people part of a loving community. The network of communities was founded by Jean Vanier in France, in 1964. He was a successful philosophy teacher, but still searching for what to do with his life. He visited an old friend who was a chaplain at a home for men with learning difficulties in Trosly. He had never met mentally handicapped people before and realised that whilst his students were concerned about bettering themselves with learning, these people simply wanted to get to know him as a person. He saw their hurts at their rejection by society and was concerned for their needs.

He bought a house in the village and invited two of the men to go and live with him. He spent his time caring for them. Other people went to help him and so the community grew. That was what he wanted to build – a community – and not an institution. He wanted handicapped people to live together, with assistants, as a unity. He said:

My idea was to create a little 'home' or family. I did not want L'Arche to be an institution but a community where each person had his or her place, where we could work, grow, celebrate and pray together.

Today the number of communities has grown hugely. There are more than ninety communities in twenty different countries, with six in Britain. Although the inspiration of each community is religious, the way that it is expressed in each will be very different. Jean Vanier is a Roman Catholic, but the British communities have become quite ecumenical. In India the communities are made up of different religions. They all grow and share and learn together.

L'Arche communities aim to show that the poor and weak among society matter. There are as many assistants as handicapped members of each community and they work together, in some cases to be self-supporting and in others to make goods that can be sold to give people a sense of pride and worth.

Jean Vanier believes that one of the most important things about working with the handicapped is that they, in fact, become the helper. They show those who would consider themselves to be 'normal' who they really are and how to become better, more loving, and accepting of people. L'Arche means 'ark'. This is a reference to the Ark of the Covenant which the Jews made to contain the stones of the Ten Commandments. They believed that it was a way of God being really present with them. In the same way, Jean Vanier believes that through the people in L'Arche communities, God is really present.

WORKSHEET 9b

PEOPLE AROUND US IN THE COMMUNITY
Handicap

1. a) Do religions care about the handicapped?
   - Find out more about the work of L'Arche communities and produce an information leaflet which might be used to advertise their work.
   - Look up Matthew 25:40. Explain how this might relate to what Jean Vanier believes about the work of L'Arche.
   - Carry out a survey of your local churches and other religious buildings. See what provision they have made for handicapped people to worship there. (For example: ramps; hearing loops; braille service books; people trained to help . . .)

   b) What conclusions can you draw? (Could you send your findings to the local churches/religious group, or to your local council?)

2. Choose one type of handicap and research more about it. Find out:
   - what effect it has on sufferers;
   - whether there is any cure or treatment;
   - what help sufferers need;
   - what organisation(s) exist to help sufferers and promote research into the handicap.

   Present your findings to each other in class so that you learn about several types of handicap.

3. Look at the case studies of Jacqueline and Ann. Choose one of them and write about the problems that she has to overcome in order to live a full life. Consider also her achievements and say why you think she has been able to do these things.

4. Many people say that handicap today can be avoided if handicapped foetuses are aborted. Although the time limit on abortions makes it difficult in some cases, it is still possible to detect handicap early on in pregnancy and to offer mothers-to-be a termination.

   a) Make notes on both sides of the argument.

   b) Use these Bible references to bring in Christian teaching.
   John 10:10b 'I have come that they may have life, and have it to the full' (Jesus)
   Romans 5:3-4 'we know that suffering produces perseverance; perseverance, character; and character, hope.' (St Paul)
   Psalm 139:16 '. . . your eyes saw my unformed body. All the days ordained for me were written in your book before one of them came to be.'
   You may be able to find other references in the Bible and other holy books too.

   c) Now debate the following:
   This house believes that it is wrong to allow handicapped babies to be born when they could be aborted, and suffering prevented.

5. If possible watch the film *The Elephant Man* and discuss the implications that it has for attitudes towards handicap. It is about a man (at the turn of the century) who was severely handicapped and the way that he was treated by those around him. At one point in the film he cries out, 'I am not an animal, I am a man'.

INFORMATION SHEET 10

PEOPLE AROUND US IN THE COMMUNITY

Living With People Around Us

This unit has looked at lots of different people. All of them put together make up the community in which we live. The unit has focused on problems faced by these people, but these problems only exist simply because they are people and are trying to live alongside other people. Every human being is unique. There are many things which divide us up and make us different to others, our: values, looks, abilities, beliefs, backgrounds, jobs, sex, race and so on.

The real challenge comes in trying to work out ways of living with the people around us so that each of us is able to live a full and purposeful life without interfering with the freedoms of others. Some people will need more of the support and help of others but we need to find ways of living, working and growing together and not just putting up with the fact that there are other people on the same planet as us!

Religions provide some ways of doing this, as they help us to focus on who we are as people, created by an all-powerful and, in the case of some religions, loving God. Religions also help to shape moral frameworks for living together so that people can know where they stand morally and in relation to others. Some people may not call themselves a follower of a religion, and yet still accept that there is a part of themselves which has a need to belong, and to be part of, the whole of creation. Others follow a well established religious faith and try to keep to the teachings of that religion.

However we look at it, we cannot deny the fact that if it were not for other people, life would not really be worth living. The challenge is to find ways of living together with those people, whether we like them all or not, and to learn from each other.